Chosen for Blessing

H.NORMAN WRIGHT

HARVEST HOUSE PUBLISHERS
Eugene, Oregon 97402

CHOSEN FOR BLESSING

Copyright © 1992 by Harvest House Publishers
Eugene, Oregon 97402

Library of Congress Cataloging-in-Publication Data

Wright, H. Norman.
  Chosen for blessing / H. Norman Wright.
  Includes bibliographical references.
  ISBN 0-89081-942-4
  1. Happiness—Religious aspects—Christianity. Christian life—1960-
3. Blessing and cursing.   I. Title.
VB4501.2.W72   1992
  248.4—dc20   92-38776
                                                                    CIP

COPY TO COME

CONTENTS

Part Four
BLESSED TO BE A BLESSING

Part One:

CHOSEN
AND
BLESSED

Chosen for His
glory!

CHAPTER ONE

Born to Be Blessed

Silence. It hung in the air like a cloud. The noise of the day had subsided, and most of the people had gone. Only a few hopefuls lingered.

One man stayed where he had been all day long. He was in no hurry to leave since he had to wait for others to take him away. And when he did leave, he did so only to go home and wait to return tomorrow. Yes, he knew he would return. He always did. It was the only hope he had. And yet he had very little hope.

The place to which he came each day was called the Pool of Bethesda. Bethesda means "house of mercy or lovingkindness." It was supposed to be a place of great blessing. No wonder it drew so many people who were lame, blind, and diseased. And those who came clung to the hope that they would receive mercy and be healed.

The lame man started coming here years ago. At first he came occasionally, then daily. The days blended into weeks, weeks became months, and months grew into years. One after another they rolled by, but he experienced no change, no blessing. After 38 years, his hope for blessing was just as crippled as his legs.

Time and time again he saw the calm surface of the pool move with a slight ripple that soon began to bubble and churn—stirred by an angel, people said. The afflicted around him rushed into the pool to submerge in the healing power they believed was present at that moment. Some people testified that God blessed them and set them free. "Why not me?" the man agonized. But day after day nothing changed. Today and tomorrow would be like yesterday. He felt unblessed (see John 5:1-9).

His story isn't unique. Many people today find themselves stuck in life, unblessed. Their hope has eroded, and they feel that life will always be this way.

I talk to people every week who feel hopeless, purposeless, and unblessed in life. And I'm not just talking about down-and-outers like the poor man at the pool. In fact, most of the people who come to me for counseling look like they have it all together. They're healthy, strong, financially stable. They have families, friends, careers, nice homes. They attend church, teach Sunday School, and sing in the choir. Yet they feel empty and unblessed. Like the man at the pool, they see others receiving God's touch of blessing and wonder why it doesn't happen to them. Perhaps some of them are just like you.

Ken sat in my office looking dejected and downtrodden. He said, "I can't figure it out, Norm. Why does God choose to bless others so much and overlook me? I feel abandoned. No matter what I try to do, it just doesn't click. Others are able to sell their homes. Mine has been on the market for 18 months. I've worked as hard as anyone else on the job for 15 years, yet I never get the big promotions. Others tell me God's blessings are right in front of me, but I sure don't see them. What do I have to do to receive His blessing?"

One woman lamented to me, "I feel so unfulfilled in my marriage. There's no excitement anymore. My husband and I maintained a pure relationship before we were married. We prayed together and were really active in church. I thought we would be happy as a married Christian couple.

But it seems like God has overlooked us. Where are all the benefits of following God's plan? Where are His blessings on our marriage? I don't understand it."

Another counselee expressed his emptiness to me by saying, "Norm, I feel like an empty jug sitting on the back shelf of life. I've been forgotten by God, and life is passing me by. I'm in a rut so deep that there isn't a ladder tall enough for me to climb out. Every day I ask God, 'Is this all there is to life?' Once I even asked Him why He lied to me. I said, 'God, you said you would bless me. Did you run out of blessings before you got to me? My Christian life isn't what you said it would be. Why?'"

Perhaps, like the people described above, you're encountering difficulties in your life that cause you to question God's plans for you. Or maybe you can't quite put your finger on the problem, but you aren't experiencing what you believe you ought to be experiencing in your relationship with the Lord. You may *look* blessed, but sometimes you don't *feel* blessed. You occasionally wonder if life has passed you by or if God has left you to flounder on your own while He is busy blessing others. And in your gnawing emptiness you ask yourself, "Have I somehow missed the purpose for my existence?"

In my counseling I have helped scores of people who felt empty and unblessed realize that God *has* blessed them and *is* blessing them. They didn't perceive His blessing because they didn't know what to look for or because something from their past was blocking their understanding of and appreciation for His blessing. I trust that the thoughts shared in these pages will help you understand, appreciate, and embrace the unsearchable riches of God's blessing in your life.

To Know and Be Known

Why were you born? Strange question? Perhaps—but who hasn't wondered? Obviously you are the product of your parents' involvement. But what else? Isn't there more to your existence than that?

Yes, there is. You were born to know God. That's why you're here. "What is the chief end of man?" the Westminster Catechism asks, and then answers, "To glorify God and to enjoy Him forever." Many people acknowledge God, but few have learned to truly know and enjoy Him, because they have a distorted images of who He is and who He created them to be. And when we have a clouded view of God and ourselves as His children, it's easy to feel that His blessing has passed us by.

The Scriptures tell us: "This is eternal life: that they may know you, the only true God, and Jesus Christ, whom you have sent" (John 17:3). Our growing knowledge of God leads to a greater realization of the goodness and grace He wants to lavish on us. The more we know about Him, the more we understand our heritage of blessing.

As we journey through life learning to know God, we discover a wonderful truth: God knows us completely and loves us just as we are. God knows you through and through. He said to Jeremiah, "Before I formed you in the womb I knew you, before you were born I set you apart" (Jeremiah 1:5). He said to Moses, "I will do the very thing you have asked, because I am pleased with you, and I know you by name" (Exodus 33:17). And Jesus said to His followers, "I am the good shepherd; I know my sheep and my sheep know me" (John 10:14).

Are we stubborn? Often. Rebellious? Sometimes. But in spite of our character traits, in spite of our doubts and fears, God has, with eyes wide open to our weaknesses, set Himself to bless us in Christ. You don't have to worry about hiding your faults from Him, because He is already fully aware of who you are, what you do, and what you think and feel.

Unfortunately, when some people hear that God knows them inside and out, their response is one of groaning or even fear. It's like the little girl who ran into her house crying after her playmate caught her doing something naughty and threatened her: "I'm going to tell God on you!" We don't have to be afraid of God's response, because nothing we ever think or do will shock God or cause Him to turn His back on us.

Perhaps the importance of being known by God is best expressed by J. I. Packer in one of the all-time classics, *Knowing God*:

> What matters supremely, therefore, is not, in the last analysis, the fact that I know God, but the larger fact which underlies it—the fact that *He knows me*. I am graven on the palms of His hands. I am never out of His mind. All my knowledge of Him depends on His sustained initiative in knowing me....
>
> There is tremendous relief in knowing that His love to me is utterly realistic, based at every point on prior knowledge of the worst about me, so that no discovery now can disillusion him about me, in the way I am so often disillusioned about myself, and quench His determination to bless me.[1]

Do these concepts generate hope within you? Do they give you a sense of security, relief, comfort? That is their purpose. You have so much more value and significance than you can possibly grasp. God has much in store for you. You have been chosen for blessing!

Let me suggest something you can do each day that will take you only two or three minutes but will help you make these thoughts part of a life-changing experience in your beliefs and attitudes. Read the paragraphs by Dr. Packer aloud morning and evening each day for the next two weeks. You may find a dozen excuses not to, but try it anyway. Give these truths an opportunity to work in your life.

The Significance of Being Chosen

God not only knows you, but He also chose you, as exemplified in the life of Abraham. Abraham was born during a time when there doesn't seem to have been much interaction going on between God and man. But one day, out of the clear blue sky, God spoke to Abraham. You can imagine what a shock it must have been, but there was no doubt: Abraham knew it was God. God said: "Leave your country, your people and your father's household and go to the land I will show you" (Genesis 12:1).

Just to be spoken to by God was a miracle. But there was more. God told Abraham that he was special. Abraham was a chosen one, the patriarch of blessing: "I will make you into a great nation and I will bless you; I will make your name great, and you will be a blessing. I will bless those who bless you, and whoever curses you I will curse; and all the peoples on earth will be blessed through you" (vv. 2-3). And since we are in Christ, we are "Abraham's seed" and heirs to the promise of blessing (Galatians 4:29).

Paul wrote, "Praise be to the God and Father of our Lord Jesus Christ, who has blessed us in the heavenly realms with every spiritual blessing in Christ. For *he chose us* in him before the creation of the world to be holy and blameless in his sight" (Ephesians 1:3-4, emphasis added). You have been chosen by God. His selection of you has nothing to do with any of your characteristics or qualities. God chose to declare you holy and blameless before Him apart from your merits and despite your shortcomings. You weren't chosen to be perfect. God simply chose you to be with Him. Why did He do this? Because He loves you.

Reflect back to a time when you were a bit younger (perhaps a *lot* younger), when you were in grade school and had to play on teams. Next to being the captain of the team, what was the best thing that could happen? Wasn't it being the first one chosen? The captain locked eyes with you, pointed his finger, and said, "I choose you." At that moment in time you knew how wonderful it was to be a chosen person. Of course, it's possible that you were never the first one chosen. Maybe you were always the very last. The good news is that those days are over. Like Abraham, you are the object of God's attention. You have a destiny. You are chosen for blessing.

In the chapters ahead, we are going to look at the blessing God has for us and the new identity we enjoy in Him. For now it's important just to see that we also have a choice. We can attempt to create our own identity and seek blessing through our own devices, or we can accept the identity and blessing God has already provided for us. Abraham accepted the identity God gave him and was blessed. As Myron Madden writes, "Abraham accepted his identity as his blessing, or you might say his blessing gave him identity."[2]

The blessing of knowing God and knowing who we are in Christ is critical to our success in life. Madden adds, "It takes the gift of blessing to help us know who we are, and we need to know that before we can say where we are going. We can't otherwise recognize our destination if we don't know our destiny."[3]

God's Pleasure over You

Our understanding of who God is and how He wants to bless our lives in enriched when we realize that He is committed to performing good in our lives. Consider God's Word: "Surely goodness and love will follow me all the days of my life, and I will dwell in the house of the Lord forever" (Psalm 23:6); "I will make an everlasting covenant with them: I will never stop doing good to them. . . . I will rejoice in doing them good and will assuredly plant them in this land with all my heart and soul" (Jeremiah 32:40-41).

A few years ago, the choir at our church sang an anthem based on Zephaniah 3:17. I had never heard the song before. The words were printed in our church bulletin, and I have read them many times since because they encourage me, inspire me, and remind me of what I mean to God:

> And the Father will dance over you in joy!
> He will take delight in whom He loves.
> Is that a choir I hear singing the praises of God?
> No, the Lord God Himself is exulting over you in song!
> And He will joy over you in song!
> My soul will make its boast in God,
> For He has answered all my cries.
> His faithfulness to me is as sure as the dawn of a
>   new day.
> Awake my soul, and sing!
> Let my spirit rejoice in God!
> Sing, O daughter of Zion, with all of your heart!
> Cast away fear for you have been restored!
> Put on the garment of praise as on a festival day.
> Join with the Father in glorious, jubilant song.
> God rejoices over you in song![4]

In his fascinating book, *The Pleasures of God*, John Piper beautifully expresses how God desires to do good to all who hope in Him. Dr. Piper talks about God singing and asks, "What would it be like if God sang?":

> What do you hear when you imagine the voice of God singing?

> I hear the booming of Niagara Falls mingled with the trickle of a mossy mountain stream. I hear the blast of Mt. St. Helens mingled with a kitten's purr. I hear the power of an East Coast hurricane and the barely audible puff of a night snow in the woods. And I hear the unimaginable roar of the sun, 865,000 miles thick, 1,300,000 times bigger than the earth, and nothing but fire, 1,000,000 degrees centigrade on the cooler surface of the corona. But I hear this unimaginable roar

mingled with the tender, warm crackling of logs in the living room on a cozy winter's night.

I stand dumfounded, staggered, speechless that he is singing over me—one who has dishonored him so many times and in so many ways. It is almost too good to be true. He is rejoicing over my good with all his heart and all his soul. He virtually breaks forth into song when he hits upon a new way to do me good.[5]

Did you catch the significance of how God feels about you and what He wants for you? Do you get a sense of the blessing for which you have been created and chosen?

Dr. Piper compares our relationship with God to a marriage. He goes on to talk about how the honeymoon ends for all married couples. Reality sets in and the level of honeymoon intensity and affection diminishes. The two people change, and defects become more apparent. But it's different with God:

God says his joy over his people is like a bridegroom over a bride. He is talking about honeymoon intensity and honeymoon pleasures and honeymoon energy and excitement and enthusiasm and enjoyment. He is trying to get into our hearts what he means when he says he rejoices over us *with all his heart.*

And to add to this, with God the honeymoon never ends. He is infinite in power and wisdom and creativity and love. And so he has no trouble sustaining a honeymoon level of intensity; he can foresee all the future quirks of our personality and has decided he will keep what's good for us and change what isn't.[6]

Does that say something to you about your value and worth? Does that fling open the doors of possibility for you to make choices in your life that will lead to hope and eventually to change and blessing? It can.

If you are searching to fill your life with meaning and significance, and you still feel empty, there is a reason. Only God's blessing will give you the inner peace and fulfillment that lasts. In the chapters ahead you will learn what the blessing of the Lord is and how to walk in that blessing. You'll also see how your experience of God's blessing on a day-to-day basis can be robbed through your own choices and how you can take risks and make changes to restore the vibrancy of your faith.

Best of all, when you begin to realize God's blessing, something will happen to your relationships with other people. You will be able to bless them because you are blessed!

Do You Want to Be Blessed?

One day Jesus arrived at the Pool of Bethesda and saw the anguished expressions of those who sat and suffered around it. Perhaps His feelings were like ours when we visit the children's ward in the hospital or a home for the handicapped or see the troubled hearts of so many of our friends. We are wrenched with sorrow, and we desire to reach out and bring a touch of healing.

Time stood still for the crippled man at the pool until Jesus came and looked at him lying on his thin straw mat. Jesus knew about his problem. He always knew. And out of His heart of concern and compassion He asked one of the strangest but most insightful questions in all of Scripture: "Do you want to get well?" (John 5:6). In effect, Jesus was extending to this man the hope of blessing. He seemed to say, "I see your hurt and helplessness, and I've come to bless you. Do you want to be blessed?"

If Jesus asked you this question at this moment in your life, what would you say? Would you answer with a resounding, "Yes!"? Would you offer a qualified, "Yes, but..."? Or would you bring up reasons why change in your life just isn't possible?

Imagine having an incurable disease and being taken to the finest clinic in the country. You meet with the top specialist in the field of your infirmity, and he says, "I can make you well. Do you want to be well?" But instead of saying yes, you give some excuse why you won't or can't be healed.

Isn't this what the man at the pool did when he told Jesus that he didn't have anyone to put him into the pool? He had come to the place in his life where he dwelt more on what couldn't happen than on what could happen, more on what wasn't possible than on what was possible.

The same thing happens to people today when facing the opportunity for blessing. Some of us have become like the man at the pool: impossibility thinkers. We miss out on so much when we respond, "It just won't happen because..."

It's so easy to respond with our own set of rehearsed excuses accumulated over the years. And often we tend to blame others for our condition: "It was my father"; "My mother is the cause of my problem"; "My negative environment and circumstances are at fault." When we blame others for who and what we are, we soon begin to feel helpless, then hopeless, and eventually resentful. And resentment is the great immobilizer. It begins to cut and sear our attitude.

Jesus didn't acknowledge the lame man's excuse. He didn't discuss it, debate it, clarify it, or seek to explain it.

If He had, would it have helped? No.

If He had, would it have hastened the change that needed to occur? No.

If He had, would it have caused the crippled man to begin to hope again? No.

It rarely does any good to fixate on the reason why we think we're unblessed. All it does is reinforce our belief that we are stuck where we are, immovably encased in cement.

Eventually the crippled man must have answered, "Yes, I want to be well," because the Master healed him. The unblessed man refused to cling to reasons why he hadn't been blessed or couldn't be blessed. He chose to reach out for the hope of blessing.

Choosing to hope and believe helps create other possibilities and alternatives. Choosing to hope can help us create changes that otherwise would never occur. Choosing to hope can help us learn to accept what might not actually change. This in itself is a change for the better. Choosing to hope is a choice for blessing. I hope you're ready to make this choice.

❦ P R A Y E R ❦

Dear Lord,

Help me remember that I have been chosen for blessing. May I experience the freedom and security that comes from the realization that I am chosen by You.

Thank You for the assurance that I belong to You. Help me think and behave as one whose life is not dependent on the approval and acceptance of others, but only on You.

Thank You for blessing me. Thank You for seeing in me the potential to be a blessing to others. Because I am affirmed by You, help my desire to bless others to grow.

In Jesus' name. Amen.

Life's Most Precious Possession

Ask a dozen people what the word blessing means and you'll probably get a dozen different answers. For many people, it means financial security. For some, it means good health. For yet others, it means meaningful relationships with significant people in their lives. Even in the Bible the word is used to express a number of different thoughts.

Are any of these phrases familiar? Have you heard them or said them yourself?

"Dear God, bless this food."

"Dear God, bless this project."

"Dear God, bless my family this coming week."

What does it mean to be "blessed"? When God blessed Abraham did something change in his life (Genesis 12:1-4)? When Jesus blessed the children were their lives richer for it (Mark 10:13-16)? We wish each other a blessed Christmas or Easter. Does something happen because we say this, or is it a meaningless tradition from earlier centuries?

Blessings have been used for thousands of years in all sorts of settings. Scripture contains numerous blessings that were spoken or written to people. For example:

May the God of peace, who through the blood of the eternal covenant brought back from the dead our Lord Jesus, that great Shepherd of the sheep, equip you with everything good for doing his will, and may he work in us what is pleasing to him, through Jesus Christ, to whom be glory for ever and ever. Amen (Hebrews 13:20-21).

Grace, mercy and peace from God the Father and from Jesus Christ, the Father's Son, will be with us in truth and love (2 John 3).

Here's a portion of a traditional blessing for newlyweds:

May Almighty God bless you by the Word of His mouth, and unite your hearts in the enduring bond of pure love.... May the peace of Christ dwell always in your hearts and in your home; may you have true friends to stand by you, both in joy and in sorrow....[1]

Here's a traditional blessing for a home:

O Lord God Almighty, bless this house. In it may there be health, chastity, victory over sin, strength, humility, goodness of heart and gentleness, full observance of your law and gratefulness to God, the Father, and the Son, and the Holy Spirit.[2]

And here's a blessing for a congregation:

The peace of God, which passes all understanding, keep your hearts and minds in the knowledge and love of God and of His Son, Jesus Christ our Lord; and the blessing of God Almighty, the Father, the Son, and the Holy Spirit, be among you and remain with you always. Amen.[3]

The words in these blessings are powerful because they touch on desires that are as common as the air we breathe. Who doesn't want peace and joy and a thousand other good things? God created us with particular needs that create a longing within us for His touch on our lives. Without this, we remain forever unsatisfied. Blessing, especially God's blessing, is life's most precious possession.

What Does It Mean to Be Blessed?

To bless generally means to speak good or to do good things for another. There are many types of blessing in Scripture. The first is the blessing *God communicates to people*. When God blessed Abraham by saying, "I will make you into a great nation and I will bless you; I will make your name great, and you will be a blessing" (Genesis 12:2), he was pronouncing a benediction promising His favor.

A second type of blessing is *spoken by people to God*. In Psalm 103:1-2, King David blesses God by saying, "Bless the Lord, O my soul; and all that is within me, bless His holy name. Bless the Lord, O my soul, and forget none of His benefits" (NASB). Speaking well of or expressing praise to God is blessing Him. When we bless Him we acknowledge Him as the source for all we have.

Yet another type is a blessing *spoken by God or people over things*. One example of this is Deuteronomy 28:4-5: "The fruit of your womb will be blessed, and the crops of your land and the young of your livestock—the calves of your herds and the lambs of your flocks. Your basket and your kneading trough will be blessed." Even in our secular age it's common in many coastal communities to have an annual blessing of the fleet ceremony at the beginning of each fishing season.

The fourth type of blessing is one *spoken by one person to another*, often invoking the name of God. When we bless someone superior to us, as when Jacob blessed Pharaoh in Genesis 47:7, the phrase suggests honoring or showing respect.[4]

The Old Testament Hebrew word for blessing means the transmission or endowment of the power of God's goodness or favor. And the Old Testament affirms that God is the source of the favor and well-being we receive. Blessing must be pretty important, because it's mentioned 415 times in the Old Testament alone.

God's blessing can be manifested in many ways. In the Old Testament, blessing often referred to fertility in procreation (Genesis 1:22,28). Repeatedly in Genesis we read God's promise to multiply Abraham's descendants to number "as the stars of heaven." The ability to bear children and leave a legacy of offspring was a primary definition of blessing at that time.

The power to defeat enemies in Old Testament times was also considered a blessing from God (Genesis 24:60; 27:29). Council and wisdom from God, leading to a successful life, was a blessing (Isaiah 9:6; 11:2). Interpersonal relationships in those days were marked by blessing. When people met and parted, they blessed each other. Mutual blessing strengthened the friendship.

There are many statements in the Old Testament that link blessing in this life to a personal relationship with God. The psalmist said people are blessed when they keep God's laws (Psalm 119:1-2), when they are disciplined by God (94:12), and when they live justly and righteously (106:3).

Sometimes blessing, related to obedience to God, was associated with physical health and material well-being. When the Law was given by God, part of its purpose was to reveal how people could live happy and fulfilled lives and avoid the misery and pain of living lives of disobedience to God (Deuteronomy 11:26-28). An individual's personal well-being was directly related to his obedient walk with God. These blessings were conditional on the individual's obedience.

Old Testament blessings were often viewed as being primarily material. If people didn't have children, land, herds, or a victorious army, they didn't feel blessed by God. Many people today feel the same way. They don't think they're blessed unless they have plenty of money, a comfortable life, and excellent health.

The Heart of Blessing

Can we experience God's blessings apart from material abundance? Yes, we can. In fact, true blessing is not simply the equivalent of prosperity, possessions, or success. In the New Testament, the word most often translated "bless" is the Greek word from which we get our words eulogy and eulogize. The word literally means to speak well of or to express praise. This kind of blessing was frequently the act of one person verbally invoking God's gracious power in another's life.

In the Beatitudes of Matthew 5, the blessings Jesus promised are basically spiritual, not material. The real rewards of blessing are found in one's relationship with God and in serving Him. Furthermore, blessing in the New Testament includes God's activity of providing our salvation through the death and resurrection of Christ.

Perhaps the most powerful picture of the core of blessing comes in the words that the Lord commanded the priests to give to the people. This familiar scriptural blessing expresses what we all inwardly long for, what we were created to receive and enjoy: God's favor. And because this blessing was given directly by God, it also expresses God's willingness and ability to perform it:

> The Lord bless you and keep you;
> the Lord make his face shine upon you and be gracious
>   to you;
> the Lord turn his face toward you and give you peace
>   (Numbers 6:24-26).

The essence of the blessing of God is the assurance that we belong to Him and that He delights in us.

God created us and keeps us day by day. We are blessed!

God redeemed us through His Son, Jesus Christ. We are blessed!

God fills us with His Spirit and equips us for life. We are blessed!

God smiles on us; He doesn't glower at us. We are blessed!

God is turned toward us, not away from us. We are blessed!

The *New International Dictionary of New Testament Theology* summarizes God's blessing this way: "If Yahweh does not hide that side of himself that is turned towards men, but lifts it up: if he does not darken it with wrath, but lets it shine; then Yahweh's blessing means his welcoming disposition towards men. The content of the blessing is described by the concepts of protection, grace and—most comprehensively—well-being."[5]

Dr. Lloyd Ogilvie says, "To be a blessed person is to know, feel, and relish God's affirmation and assurance, acceptance, and approval. It is the experience of being chosen and cherished, valued and enjoyed."[6]

In the Old Testament this assurance belonged to the children of Israel, the linear descendants of Abraham and God's "chosen people." In the New Testament it belongs to everyone who receives Jesus Christ by faith: "He [Jesus] redeemed us in order that the blessing given to Abraham might come to the Gentiles through Christ Jesus, so that by faith we might receive the promise of the Spirit" (Galatians 3:14). You belong to God through Christ. He delights in you. You are blessed!

How important is the blessing of God in our lives? Can we live without it? No. As Dr. Ogilvie states:

We all need [blessing] desperately. It is the one great need we all share in common. We were born for it and there is no lasting joy without it. What oxygen is for the lungs and protein for the body, that is what it is for our souls....With it we become winsome and free; without it we are willful and fearful. It is the one thing people most need from us, but the one thing we cannot give until we have received it. It is life's most precious possession.[7]

You may be saying, "Norm, you seem to be talking about two kinds of blessing. I hear you say we are blessed because of who we are in Christ. And I hear you say we are blessed when we obey God in our daily lives. Which is the correct definition of blessing?"

Both are correct. However, one is primary, and the other is secondary. When you placed your faith in Jesus Christ as your Savior, you were blessed "in the heavenly realms with every spiritual blessing in Christ" (Ephesians 1:3). Your spiritual blessings in Christ are secure and constant. You are blessed with eternal life (John 3:16). You are blessed with a loving relationship with God (John 1:12). Your name is written in the Lamb's book of life (Revelation 3:5; 21-27). Spiritual blessings are first and foremost.

No matter how well or how poorly you perform as a Christian, these blessings cannot be diminished or taken away. Abraham, for example, wasn't always obedient to God, but he was eternally blessed because he believed God (Romans 4:1-3). You aren't always obedient either, but if you have received God's grace through faith in Christ, you are always blessed (Ephesians 2:8-9). This assurance that we belong to God and are eternally blessed in Him is the central focus of this book.

But there are additional blessings to be received and enjoyed, and they are realized through our obedience to God. As Christians we have been called to obedience, and when we fail to obey God we miss out on the daily blessings God is prepared to pour out upon us. Jesus concluded His teaching ministry to His disciples by saying, "Now that you know these things, you will be blessed if you do them" (John 13:17); "If you obey my commands, you will remain in my love, just as I have obeyed my Father's commands and remain in his love. I have told you this so that my joy may be in you and that your joy may be complete" (John 15:10-11).

You are already blessed by being in Christ; but you will experience greater blessing and joy by walking obediently in Christ. This doesn't mean that you will be wealthy, healthy, and pain-free all your life. Rather, obedience is the doorway to receiving the blessing of God's provision no matter what state you may be in materially or physically. Obedience brings the blessing of great peace. Roger Palms writes, "The ones who are surrendered in obedience to Jesus Christ can relax and live and enjoy themselves whether they have much or very little—because logically, sensibly, through good counsel and with prayer, they are doing what they know God has asked them to do."[8]

There is fulfillment in being obedient. We discover that we no longer have to live up to the expectations of others or to compete with the world's standards. There is freedom in being obedient. Our sense of security, satisfaction, contentment, and happiness increases with our growth in obedience. Years ago, Thomas Kelly wrote, "The life that intends to be wholly obedient, wholly submissive, wholly listening is astonishing in its completeness. Its joys are ravishing, its peace profound, its humility the deepest, its power world-shaking, its love enveloping, its simplicity that of a trusting child. It is the life in which the prophets and apostles lived. It is the life and power of Jesus."[9]

Looking for Blessing in All the Wrong Places

When people feel unblessed by God, they often embark on a frantic search to fill the void in their lives by seeking acceptance and approval of other people. This striving is often prompted by a persistent fear of rejection that causes approval seekers to compromise who they really are. Like Esau who sold his birthright for a bowl of lentil stew, they forfeit a greater good in order to gain temporary relief from their distress.

Many approval addicts believe, "If I am accepted by others, I will be satisfied and blessed, and my life will be fulfilled." But no experience of human approval leads to permanent satisfaction. Every acceptance episode soon wears off, and the fear of rejection returns with a stronger craving for approval.

In reality, we all have varied needs for approval, and the intensity of these needs fluctuates. You may not be an approval addict in the sense that you can handle most rejections quite well. But a few rejections—especially from those who are significant to you—can crush and devastate you.

For those who are addicted to the approval and acceptance of others, there is a high price to pay. The price tag includes an extreme vulnerability to the whims and subjective opinions of the people around you. Others can take advantage of your vulnerability and mistreat you, which leads to additional rejection.

Those fearing rejection may also appear shy, timid, or ill at ease around others. These people seem to dodge close relationships, often commenting, "Who needs other people?" But many times their words can be translated, "I'm afraid of being rejected." Some people may appear cool, aloof, superior, distant, or indifferent. What is the end result of this behavior? No relationships, no blessings received through others, and no blessings given to others.

When we seek to fulfill our lives by depending on other people's perceptions of ourselves, we shut off God's blessing and His affirmation in our daily experience. And that makes it hard to pass blessings on to others. I see this on the part of husbands neglecting to affirm their wives,

wives neglecting to affirm their husbands, and parents neglecting to affirm their children. The legacy we pass on to these other unaffirmed people is an emptiness that in turn causes them also to seek affirmation in the wrong places—and the vicious cycle continues!

A Passion for Blessing

Jacob was a man who started off in life seeking blessing in the wrong places. He was insecure, restless, and strong-willed. His brother Esau, as the firstborn, was the primary heir to his father's possessions. In his quest for blessing, Jacob finagled Esau into selling his birthright for a bowl of stew (Genesis 25:29-34). Later Jacob, with his mother Rebekeh's help, stole Esau's blessing from their aging father Isaac (Genesis 27). But he still felt empty, unblessed.

What Jacob really wanted was God's blessing. In a dream God gave Jacob an assurance: "I am the Lord, the God of your father Abraham and the God of Isaac; the land on which you lie, I will give it to you and your descendants. . . . In you and in your descendants shall all the families of the earth be blessed. . . . I will not leave you until I have done what I have promised you" (Genesis 28:13-15, NASB).

If ever there was a man who wanted blessing, it was Jacob. His hunger for blessing was undeniable. Finally in Genesis 32 we read the encounter of Jacob's wrestling match with God. He would not let go until God blessed him. After his face-to-face meeting with God, Jacob, renamed Israel, was a changed person. Finally his identity was secure. Finally the fear was gone. Finally he could face his guilt as he approached his brother. Why? Because of the touch of God on his life—because of God's blessing.

Just like Jacob, we all need the fullness of God to fill our emptiness. Sometimes I talk with people who feel as though they don't deserve God's blessing. Well, we don't. Just like we do not deserve the grace of God. God gives it to us anyway; that's what makes it grace. Remember: There is nothing we have done or can do to deserve God's favor, God's delight, God's smile of blessing. *It is God's nature to bless us!* Did you hear that? *It is God's nature to bless us!*

Jesus said, "Do not be afraid, little flock, for your Father has been pleased to give you the kingdom" (Luke 12:32); "If you, then, though you are evil, know how to give good gifts to your children, how much more will your Father in heaven give good gifts to those who ask him!" (Matthew 7:11). Paul wrote, "He redeemed us in order that the blessing given to Abraham might come to the Gentiles through Christ Jesus, so that by faith we might receive the promise of the Spirit" (Galatians 3:14); "Praise be to the God and Father of our Lord Jesus Christ, who has blessed us in the heavenly realms with every spiritual blessing in Christ" (Ephesians 1:3). God has chosen you, God is with you, God favors you. His blessing is yours to receive and enjoy.

A primary evidence of God's blessing in our lives is who we have become in Christ. In the next chapter we will talk about our identity as blessed ones of the Father.

🎄 P R A Y E R 🎄

Dear Lord,

Thank You for not withholding Your blessing until I deserve it. Thank You that the heart of Your blessing is the assurance that I belong to You in Christ and that You delight in me. Thank You for smiling on me and turning toward me.

Help me not to seek Your blessing in the wrong places. I want to live my life addicted to your approval, not the approval of others. Create in me a passion for Your blessing. I want to bask daily in the blessing that is Your nature.

In Jesus' name. Amen.

(May 1, 2013)

CHAPTER THREE

You Really Are Special

We live in a time of fragile identities. I hear people make statements like:

• "I'm the president of a large company." (But the next week he filed for bankruptcy.)

• "I'm the coach of a winning college football team." (But this season the team lost six games, and he lost his job.)

• "I'm a model for a large department store chain." (But she was suddenly replaced by a model half her age.)

• "I'm a mother." (Yet this past year one child died and another ran away from home and hasn't been heard from since.)

• "I'm a concert pianist." (Two fingers were severed in an accident five days ago.)

So what happens to their identity now? Does it shatter? Was it too fragile? Was it built on society's standards? Did it have a base that would withstand the sudden and unexpected earthquakes of life?

At one of my seminars I ask people to introduce themselves to those around them without mentioning what they do for a living. Many of them are frustrated because their identity is based primarily in what they do—their job, their role in the family, their role in the church.

Would you be frustrated too? Is your identity based on the physical and material elements of your existence? Are you someone who ought to wear a sign that says, "Fragile. Handle with care. I break easier than you think"? Not sure? Think about these questions:

• Who will you be when you are no longer a spouse or a parent?

• Who will you be when you are no longer an executive, a social worker, a minister, a carpenter, a clerk, an athlete?

• Who will you be when you can no longer run or walk?

If we have no sense of who we are beyond our physical abilities and roles in life, we have confined ourselves to a state of identity confusion. And when we're confused about who we are, it's hard to walk in the blessing of God.

What's at the Heart of Who You Are?

You can avoid this confusion by determining what you have based your identity on. Ask yourself these questions:

• To whom are you attached (spouse, parent, mentor, friend, etc.) who most deeply influences your identity?

• What things are you attached to that influence your identity? For example, how important is your house, your job, your community standing, your car, or your wardrobe as sources for your identity?

• What about your appearance? Does your identity fluctuate based on how good you think you look?

• What about your performance? Does how you feel about yourself fluctuate based on how well you do as a spouse, a parent, or an employer/employee?

Whenever we build our identity on anything that is potentially changeable, what do you think it does to our identity? It makes us prone to experiencing not only the changes and losses themselves but the potential loss of our identity as well.[1]

I've met beautiful women and handsome men who feel like nobodies—no real identity.

I've known wealthy men and women of all ages who feel like nobodies—no real identity.

I've seen men and women with power and prestige who feel like nobodies—no real identity.

From the world's standpoint, these people have everything. But it doesn't matter. What they really want eludes them—their identity. They all feel like the person in this song:

> If I were a cloud, I'd sit and cry,
> If I were the sun, I'd sit and sigh,
> But I'm not a cloud, nor am I the sun,
> I'm just sitting here, being no one.
>
> If I were the wind, I'd blow here and there,
> If I were the rain, I'd fall everywhere,
> But I'm not the wind, nor am I the rain,
> I'm just no one—feeling pain.
>
> If I were the snow, I'd fall oh so gently,
> If I were the sea, waves would roll o'er me,
> But I'm not the snow, nor am I the sea,
> I'm just no one....[2]

In order to truly appreciate that we belong to God, that He loves us unconditionally in Christ, and that He smiles on us daily, we need to gain a deeper understanding of who we are and what we are becoming as His children. Let's consider several sections from Ephesians 1 that describe our identity in God's family.

You're in the Family

We have already talked about the good news in Ephesians 1:3-4 that God has blessed us eternally in Christ by choosing us to be His. Verse 4 tells us how close our relationship with God is: "In love he predestined us to be adopted as his sons through Jesus Christ." You're not a stranger to God. You're not even a distant relative. God has chosen you to be His child. You are blessed!

Imagine that you are standing outside your church one Sunday morning after the service and a visitor approaches you and says, "By the way, did you know that you and I came from the same adoption agency? When were you adopted?"

Now I can imagine a number of ways you might respond to this person. One response would be surprise as you wonder which planet this stranger just flew in from. You might even say, "I don't know what you're talking about. I wasn't adopted. I grew up with my natural parents, and they're still living. And you and I certainly didn't come from the same family."

The stranger replies, "But it's true. We are from the same adopted family. When were you adopted?"

In reality, both of you are correct, but you're talking about two different experiences. If you both know Jesus Christ as Savior, you were both adopted into God's family. The apostle John wrote: "To all who received him, to those who believed in his name, he gave the right to become children of God" (John 1:12). Romans 8:16 states: "The Spirit himself testifies with our spirit that we are God's children." Understanding the fullness of your spiritual adoption can redirect your thinking and response to life. Your adoption is a gift of grace. This is how you have been chosen for blessing.

In Roman law during New Testament times it was common practice for a childless adult who wanted an heir to adopt an adult male as his son. We too have been adopted by God as His heirs. The apostle Paul wrote: "Now if we are children, then we are heirs—heirs of God and co-heirs with Christ" (Romans 8:17); "So you are no longer a slave, but a son; and since you are a son, God has made you also an heir" (Galatians 4:7).

Do you remember the movie *Ben Hur*? Judah Ben Hur was a Jewish slave until the Roman admiral, Arias, adopted him. Judah was given all the rights and privileges of full sonship. He was accepted by Arias as if he had been born into the family. Similarly, when you received Jesus Christ as your Savior, you were adopted into God's family and received all the rights and privileges of a full heir. You are blessed!

What are some of the rights and privilege you inherited? Ephesians lists many of them:

• You have been guaranteed eternal life, as evidenced by the presence of the Holy Spirit in your life (1:14).

• You have hope in Christ, your glorious inheritance (1:18).

• You have experienced the incomparable power that raised Jesus Christ from the dead and seated Him at God's right hand (1:19-20).

• You are the recipient of God's incomparable grace that saved you apart from anything you have done or can ever do (2:8-9).

• You now have access to the Father through His Spirit (2:18).

• You can know the love of Christ which will enable you to receive God's fullness (3:19).

I have worked with a number of clients who were physically adopted as children. They have shared with me how they felt when they first learned that they were adopted. Some were delighted to know that someone cared enough about them to select them. But others were angry and resentful toward their natural parents for abandoning them. Some were upset at both sets of parents.

How do you feel about being adopted by the King of the universe and being delivered from the kingdom of darkness (Colossians 1:13)? This is one of the greatest blessings that the gospel offers you. You have been taken into God's family and fellowship, and you have been established as His child and heir. You may have come from a dysfunctional home and perhaps experienced emotional or physical abuse in your natural family. But God is a Father who can fill the gaps in your life because of who He is and what He has done for you. And because you are in a family, closeness, affection, and generosity are the basis of your relationship with Father God. You are loved and cared for by your Father. Your relationship as an heir is the basis for your Christian life and the foundation for all of the other blessings you receive in your day-to-day experience.

Our relationship as adopted children of God has a number of implications for the way we live our lives. Just as a child grows up imitating its father and mother, so we can become more and more like our Father God.

We see this, for example, in the Sermon on the Mount in which Christ calls us to *imitate* our Father: "Love your enemies and pray for those who persecute you....Be perfect, therefore, as your heavenly Father is perfect" (Matthew 5:44,48).

We are also called to *glorify* our Father: "Let your light shine before men, that they may see your good deeds and praise your Father in heaven" (Matthew 5:16).

We are called to *please* our Father: "When you give to the needy, do not let your left hand know what your right hand is doing, so that your giving may be in secret. Then your Father, who sees what is done in secret, will reward you.... When you pray, go into your room, close the door and pray to your Father, who is unseen. Then your Father, who sees what is done in secret, will reward you" (Matthew 6:3-4,6).

As we imitate, glorify, and please our Father, we begin to sense the thrill of participating in the destiny for which we were created. We not only enjoy the blessing of *being* God's children, we realize the personal benefits that come from *behaving* as God's children. Our knowledge of God grows, as does our awareness of His knowledge and love for us. As we live out our identity as God's adopted children day by day, we are personally transformed. We are blessed with the understanding that we are fulfilling our purpose in life.

You are Forgiven and Secured by God

Not only is your blessing based on being chosen and adopted by God, when asked who you are you can reply, "I am a forgiven person." The death of Jesus Christ was the complete payment for everything you have done wrong: "In him we have redemption through his blood, the forgiveness of sins, in accordance with the riches of God's grace.... Having believed, you were marked in him with a seal, the promised Holy Spirit, who is a deposit guaranteeing our inheritance" (Ephesians 1:7,13,14).

It's not that God decided just to excuse our sins and say, "No problem. I'll just dismiss the charges." No. The penalty for our sins had to be paid. God spared nothing to secure for you an eternal identity in Christ. He willingly gave His cherished Son in order to give you the right to be with Him forever. Not only that, you are safe in His care forever.

Perhaps the best way to explain the security we enjoy is to describe how I feel when I go to my bank and ask to see my safety deposit box. I have to sign in to prove my ownership, have my signature evaluated, and produce the proper key. Only then will the attendant take out the bank's key and use both keys to let me see my box.

When I leave, my box is locked up and the outer doors of the safe are locked as well. I go away feeling comfortable and confident that my valuables are well protected. I rest assured that they will always be there whenever I need them.

Of course, my sense of security is based on human standards and structures. Unfortunately, human measures of security have their limitations. Even the most securely guarded banks and locked vaults can be robbed.

But there is a spiritual security we share that has no limitations. There is a word used in this passage that we don't usually use: sealed. To the readers of Paul's day, the term was significant. The seal of Rome signified ownership and security. The tomb of Jesus was sealed (Matthew 27:65-66). At that time in history, the seal was the ultimate sign of security, and people relied upon it for security and authority. Unfortunately, the seal of the Roman empire wasn't indestructible. It could be broken just like my safety deposit box can be broken into by some clever criminal.

But you and I have been *sealed* by the Holy Spirit, and we are totally secure in Jesus Christ. We have been purchased by the blood of Christ. God owns me. If you have surrendered your life to Jesus Christ, then God owns you. You don't have to be concerned about being tossed out, kicked out, rejected, or dropped. You have been permanently sealed as God's possession. Paul wrote: "I am convinced that neither death nor life, neither angels nor demons, neither the present nor the future, nor any powers, neither height nor depth, nor anything else in all creation, will be able to separate us from the love of God that is in Christ Jesus our Lord" (Romans 8:38-39). How blessed we are to be secure in Christ!

You are Under New Management

When you became a Christian, you became somebody. You became a new species. Your body didn't change. Your hair and eye color didn't change. You look the same and may feel the same. But you are not the same. You are a different person. Your new identity came into being at that time. You are a "new creation" (2 Corinthians 5:17). You are "God's workmanship, created in Christ Jesus" (Ephesians 2:10).

Perhaps the best way to describe your new identity is through the concept of a company. This company is a profit-making company whose sole purpose is to generate money for the stockholders and show a steady profit. Every employee has this goal as their purpose. Seminars are held constantly for the sales personnel so they can increase their sales. Financial analysts work with the figures and the business plan to extract the greatest level of efficiency possible from each person and department.

One day the full ownership of the company changes hands. It becomes a brand new company with new leadership and a new purpose. And the new direction is to serve people rather than make money. The company's new aim is to look at the needs of the world and do something to help those who are suffering and needy. So the transition from the old way of doing business to the new way happens smoothly, right?

Wrong. All of the company's personnel, procedures, and methods of operation have been geared to the profit-making mode. Their old criteria for success is deeply ingrained. It's time to reeducate everyone in the company. Their attitudes, beliefs, and behaviors need renovation. Even the computers need to be reprogrammed. The core of the company has changed, but this change needs to permeate every facet of the company.

The same is true of us. Before we became Christians we lived by a deeply ingrained set of rules designed to help us get the most out of life. We were living for ourselves, not for God, and that's called sin. When we accepted Jesus Christ we gained a totally new identity that is to be expressed in a totally new lifestyle. We are brand new inside, but we must allow our new identity to permeate our old habits and thoughts and change our behavior. As Romans 6:11 states, "Consider yourselves to be dead to sin, but alive to God in Christ Jesus" (NASB).

We have new directives from the new management. Romans 6 describes it well: "Our old self was crucified with him so that the body of sin might be [rendered powerless], that we should no longer be slaves to sin" (Romans 6:6).[3]

Mike and Tim were sitting in a restaurant talking. Tim had just become a believer in Jesus Christ the week before. Mike was illustrating the Christian life as a company under new management. The concept made sense to Tim because he was involved in a large company. He had also built his personal identity on a false foundation.

After a while Tim asked, "By the way, what are some of the new directions that I need to operate under? What does Christ, my new manager, want me to do?"

Mike took out his Bible and said, "Let me just share a few of them with you. Some may be a bit foreign to you, but they work. God's directions are the best way to live life. God has blessed you with salvation. Here's how He wants you to bless Him and others. Listen." Then Mike read these verses from Romans 12:9-18 (TLB):

> Don't just pretend that you love others: really love them. Hate what is wrong. Stand on the side of the good. Love each other with brotherly affection and take delight in honoring each other. Never be lazy in your work but serve the Lord enthusiastically.
>
> Be glad for all God is planning for you. Be patient in trouble, and prayerful always. When God's children are in need, you be the one to help them out. And get into the habit of inviting guests home for dinner or, if they need lodging, for the night.
>
> If someone mistreats you because you are a Christian, don't curse him; pray that God will bless him. When others are happy, be happy with them. If they are sad, share their sorrow. Work happily together. Don't try to act big. Don't try to get into the good graces of important people, but enjoy the company of ordinary folks And don't think you know it all!

Never pay back evil for evil. Do things in such a way that everyone can see you are honest clear through. Don't quarrel with anyone. Be at peace with everyone, just as much as possible.

Saturated with Blessing

How can we grasp all the truths about who we are in Jesus Christ? How is it possible to counter the constant bombardment of our own negative messages from the past and what we hear in our daily lives about who we are, who we should become, or what we should do? There is a way. It's summed up in this phrase: Saturate yourself with the truth of your new identity in Christ.

Strange answer? Perhaps.

Different concept? Yes.

Does it work? Yes!

Your old, strictly human identity was molded over time in figurative concrete with a great deal of reinforcement. But alterations can occur. When you soak up the truth of who God is, what He has done for you, and who you are as a result, you will begin to be different.

In war, saturation bombing is often used to totally obliterate enemy positions in certain areas. Planes continuously drop load after load of bombs in a back-and-forth, crisscross pattern until every inch of land has been covered. Similarly, you need to allow the Holy Spirit to saturate every inch of your heart and mind with the blessed truth of who you are and what you are becoming in Christ.

Years ago I was fishing in a lake with one of my shelties. He was perched on the bow of the boat and enjoying riding along with his nose in the wind. I was headed into a cove at full speed, then I suddenly changed my mind about fishing there, swung the boat around, and reversed direction. The sudden course change caused my dog to lose his balance, and he went flying into the lake. I don't know who was more surprised; my sheltie or me!

I swung the boat around to where he was swimming (he wasn't too happy with me at that moment) and cut the engine. I picked him out of the water, but I didn't bring him into the boat right away because he was totally soaked. There wasn't a dry spot of fur or skin on him. I held him away from the boat and gently squeezed his coat to eliminate most of the water.

My new dog is quite different. For one thing, he weighs three times as much as my sheltie did. And since he's a golden retriever, he loves playing in the water, but he doesn't get soaked. His coat actually repels the water. When he comes out of the water he appears wet, but the water doesn't penetrate his thick coat. After a short time it doesn't even seem like he ever went swimming.

Some of us are thick-coated like my retriever, but in a negative way. God's truth has never thoroughly penetrated our outer layer and deeply influenced us. We haven't been fully soaked. We're not saturated with the blessing of our identity in Christ. But for growth to occur, you must saturate yourself in God's truth. How? Time and time again you will read the same instruction in this book: Take a Scripture verse or a thought we have been discussing, write it on an index card, and read it out loud to yourself morning and evening for three to four weeks. Spend time praying over the verse or thought, asking God to help you capture the vision of how it is to be manifested and reflected in your life. Envision yourself living out what you have read. Commit yourself by God's power to take steps to do what it says. You *will* be different.

So who are you? A new person, a special person, a person under new management. You have been chosen for blessing.

❧ *P R A Y E R* ❧

Dear Lord,

I praise you for Your act of choosing me, adopting me, and making me Your heir. Thank You for forgiving my sin and sealing me with Your Holy Spirit.

Thank You that I am never out of Your mind.

Thank You for not being disillusioned about me.

Thank You for Your continuing determination to bless me.

Thank You for the never ending joy You have over me.

Saturate me with the truth of who You are and what I am becoming because of my identity in You.

I know there are times when I disappoint myself and others, and this causes me to wonder how Your love and acceptance can be so constant.

But I pray that the way I live my life will reflect the value You place on me. I pray that I will draw others to open their lives to You. May they be able to discover what You have done for them.

In Jesus' name. Amen.

Part Two:

"BUT I DON'T *FEEL* BLESSED"

CHAPTER FOUR

Dealing with Distorted Images from the Past

Peter was shocked. He'd been called a lot of things in his lifetime. A smelly fisherman. A menial laborer. A fanatic. But he'd never been called a rock. Nobody had ever referred to him as a man of authority. Nobody had ever told him he would lead a heavenly charge through the gates of hell. But Jesus just did (see Matthew 16:17-20).

Peter probably thought, *Does He know who He's talking to? Does He have me confused with someone else? Or does He know something about me that nobody else knows? Something that I don't even know?*

This fisherman was having a major identity crisis. He had an idea who Jesus was. And he thought he knew who he was. But Jesus was saying some things about him that sounded too good to be true. If they could only be true. He would be so blessed. Of course, they *were* true. And he *was* blessed. It was Peter's perception that needed to be corrected.

Jesus does with each of us what He did with Peter. He makes us a new creation and gives us a new nature. He gives meaning to our lives. Acknowledging our true identity is a key to realizing our blessing. If you are concerned about who you are and what you can become, you need to get a true picture of your identity in Christ as God's child.

49

Our identity in Him is solid.

It's non-erosive.

It's permanent.

It fills the void within us.

It's the foundation of God's blessing in our lives.

As we saw in the last chapter, even though we have a new nature and a new identity in Christ, we still carry with us distorted images of ourselves and God from the past. Sometimes it helps to look at the ways our old nature was nurtured so that we can understand more clearly why the past sometimes blocks the blessing of daily, loving, welcoming fellowship with God.

Who Shaped Your Identity?

As we move through childhood and adolescence, we are influenced by many different people: parents, siblings, teachers, ministers, and friends. The character traits of these significant people have a profound effect on us and our sense of identity. Those people who displayed positive traits in our lives made it easy for us to feel accepted and blessed. Those who clouded our lives with negative traits caused us to doubt that we could ever be chosen for blessing.

Take a few minutes and consider the people in your life who *most* typified each of the traits on the following pages. You may think of more than one person for each trait, but for now write the name of the one person who most reflected each trait. Then in the space provided indicate how this person actually demonstrated this trait toward you.

Which negative influences from the list above tend to hinder you most as you attempt to embrace your identity in Christ and enjoy His blessing? Make these items matters of personal prayer and prayer with your spouse or close Christian friends.

Trait	Person/relationship	How trait demonstrated
Gentle		
Stern		
Loving		
Disapproving		
Distant		
Close and intimate		
Kind		
Angry		
Demanding		
Supportive		
Disciplining		
Gracious		
Harsh		
Wise		
Holy		
Leader		
Provider		

Trait	Person/relationship	How trait demonstrated
Trustworthy		
Joyful		
Forgiving		
Good		
Cherishing of me		
Compassionate		
Impatient		
Unreasonable		
Strong		
Protective		
Passive		
Encouraging		
Sensitive		
Just		
Unpredictable[1]		

Distorted Images of God

When we evaluate our relationship with God, we can begin to see how our perception of Him and His blessing has been influenced by our relationships with others. The inventory on the following pages will help you pinpoint some of your feelings about God and understand why your sense of identity and blessing may be distorted. This exercise is subjective; there are no right or wrong answers. To ensure that it reveals your actual feelings, please follow the instructions carefully.

1. Complete each part openly and honestly. Some people feel that God may be displeased if they give a negative answer. Nothing is further from the truth. He is pleased with our honesty. A foundation of transparency is required for growth to occur.

2. Don't respond from a theological knowledge of God but from your personal experience.

3. Don't describe what your relationship with God *ought* to be or what you *hope* it will be but what it is right now.

4. Turn each character trait into a question. For example: "To what degree do I really feel that God is gentle with me?"; "To what degree do I really feel that God is stern with me?"; etc.

5. For each trait, answer this question: "In what way do I perceive this trait in God?" Write your responses in the "Example" column.

It's so easy to hold a distorted view of God. Too often, non-Christians and many Christians as well create their own image of God based on their past experiences. We project onto God our own expectations and perceptions of who He should be and what He should do for us. And to the extent that we allow our view of God to be distorted, to that extent our experience of His blessing is limited.

To what degree do I really feel that God is…

Trait	Always	Very often	Sometimes	Hardly ever	Never	Don't know	Example
Gentle							
Stern							
Loving							
Aloof							
Disapproving							
Distant							
Close and intimate							
Kind							
Angry							
Caring							
Demanding							
Supportive							
Interested							
Disciplining							
Gracious							

Harsh
Wise
Holy
Leader
Provider
Trustworthy
Joyful
Forgiving
Good
Cherishing of me
Compassionate
Impatient
Unreasonable
Strong
Protective
Passive
Encouraging
Sensitive
Just
Unpredictable[2]

Sometimes we create our personal God in response to the good or bad traits of people who are significant in our lives. The authors of *Mistaken Identity* write, "No child arrives at the 'house of God' without his pet God under his arm. For some of us the 'pet God' we have tied on a leash to our hearts is not very nice, nor is it biblically accurate. This is because our negative images of God are often rooted in our emotional hurts and the destructive patterns of relating to people that we carry with us from our past."[1]

We imagine that God will respond to us in the very same way that our parents, siblings, or friends have. We may know differently in our head, but too often our emotional side overrides what we know.

We're not alone in fashioning a false God from our experiences with people. There were those in Scripture who did the same. Job was one of them. During the depth of his difficulties his words revealed that he wasn't seeing God accurately:

> Even if I summoned [God]... I do not believe he would give me a hearing. He would crush me with a storm and multiply my wounds for no reason (Job 9:16-17).

> You write down bitter things against me (13:26).

> You destroy [my] hope (14:19).

> God assails me and tears me in his anger and gnashes his teeth at me; my opponent fastens on me his piercing eyes.... All was well with me, but he shattered me (16:9,12).

> God has made me a byword to everyone, a man in whose face people spit (17:6).

> God has wronged me.... He has stripped me of my honor and removed the crown from my head.... He has alienated my brothers from me; my acquaintances are completely estranged from me (19:6,9,13).

I cry out to you, O God, but you do not answer; I stand up, but you merely look at me (30:20).

But Job persisted in trusting God, and later his perception came back into line with the reality of who God is.

It is best to develop our concept of God from the Scriptures rather than from our earthly relationships. Knowing God for who He really is is vital to experiencing His blessing.

Growing into God's Blessing

Do you know what happens when you have a proper picture and understanding of God? You begin to get a proper picture and understanding of yourself. You can grow. You can be changed. You can be blessed.

In order to gain a clearer perception of God and how He wants to bless your life, read each statement below and then describe how you feel about it.

God is patient and available. He has chosen to spend time and attention on you (2 Peter 3:9).

God is kind and gracious on your behalf. He has chosen to bring help and intervention into your life (Psalm 103:8).

God will work all things for your good. God desires to give you His support and encouragement. You can trust Him (Romans 8:28).

God values you as His child. He is constantly affirming and building you up. You have value because He created you and because you are in Christ (John 1:12).

God has included you in His family. You now belong to Him (Ephesians 1:4-5).

God desires intimate fellowship with you. You are valuable and priceless in His eyes (Revelation 3:20).

God loves you just as you are. You don't have to try to earn His love (Ephesians 2:8-9).

God accepts you regardless of your performance. He sees who you are more than what you do (Psalm 103:8-10).

God forgives you for your sins and failures and does not hold them against you. You can be trusted to do right and to come to Him when you've done wrong, knowing that He has chosen to forgive you (1 John 1:9).

God is just, holy, and fair. He will treat you fairly and, when He disciplines you, it will be done in love and for your own good (Hebrews 12:5-8).

God is reliable and is with you always. He will stick by you and support you (Lamentations 3:22-23).[2]

Do you struggle with feelings that you're unblessed because of distorted images of yourself and God from the past? Here's an exercise that will help you shed those false perceptions and appreciate your true identity and God's true nature. Write each of the statements above, including the Scripture verses, on an index card. Read this set of cards aloud to yourself each day for 2-3 weeks. You'll be amazed at how your perception of God and yourself begins to change as you flood your mind with God's truth.

Are you blessed? Yes.

Are you aware of all of the blessings available? Probably not.

Are you aware of all of the blessings you have received? Probably not.

But you are a person chosen for blessing.

Discover it!

Experience it!

Share it!

🍂 *P R A Y E R* 🍂

Dear Lord,

I'm thankful that there is no question about who You are. Your attributes and Your work here on Earth give me the certainty that I can come to know who I am and that I have value in Your eyes.

I ask You to help me discover the fragile bases upon which I have built who I am. Loosen my hold on these and strengthen my grip on the foundation that You have established for me.

I want to enjoy You. This is a new thought for me. But I don't want to just know You and glorify You but to delight in You as well.

And thank You that I have been chosen for blessing.

In Jesus' name. Amen.

CHAPTER FIVE

Are You a Yesterday Person?

S he was shaped so oddly. People didn't bother to stare at her anymore. They had grown accustomed to the way she looked. It seemed as though she had been that way forever. At least it was like forever to her. Not being able to straighten up for a few hours is inconvenient. But being bent over day after day for 18 years is agony.

She was always conscious of her misshapen back. Some of the muscles were limp, and others were over-developed to carry her twisted form. She learned long ago not to fight against the crippling deformity. It didn't do any good to fight it. It just pained her more.

After 18 years she just existed day to day. Her infirmity was her past, present, and future. There was no distinction for her. Each day blended into the next. Why should tomorrow be any different? It's just a continuation of yesterday. It's predetermined.

But Jesus broke the bondage of the years of pain and awkward adjustments for this woman. She didn't ask for freedom from her ailment. She wasn't seeking it. Jesus didn't even bother to ask her if she wanted it. Perhaps He just looked out over the crowd, and His heart was touched by compassion because of what He saw. Maybe this is how it happened.

Jesus closes the scroll he's been teaching from and bids her to come to the front of the synagogue. It is an embarrassing moment for the woman. All eyes are riveted to her angular body as she makes her way awkwardly down the aisle.

She stops before him, twisting her torso in a strained attempt to see his face, and their eyes meet.

"Woman, you are freed from your sickness."

Jesus lays his hands on her hunched-over shoulders. And immediately the fisted muscles release their grip, the vertebrae fall into place, and the captive nerves are set free.

Like a cat arising from too long a nap, she stretches herself erect. As she does, 18 years of misery tumble from her back to fall at the Savior's feet.[1]

Her past no longer burdened her present or threatened her future. She didn't have to carry the excess baggage anymore. She was free. Jesus set her free (see Luke 13:10-13).

Caught in the Quicksand of the Past

We are children of God, chosen for blessing. We are destined to walk through life with our heads held high, confident in the assurance that we belong to God and that He is being reflected in the way we live our lives. But sometimes we are crippled in our Christian life not only by a distorted image of God and of ourselves, but by experiences from the past. Much like the woman in Luke 13 was crippled by her physical condition, we exist, we can function, we understand our *eternal* destiny. But we're far from living a life of blessing in the here-and-now.

I remember a time when I was fishing the Snake River with a friend. We had been walking the river for about an hour when we found a place where two channels of the river converged—an ideal spot to fish. Since both my friend and I had waders on, we could walk through the water to any spot we chose. He chose to stand near the bank, and I headed out to a spot where the two channels came together.

As I stood there casting into the frothy water, I noticed that my feet were settling a bit deeper into the mud and sand. I didn't think much about it, but every time I cast and shifted my weight, I sank a little deeper into the river bed. But when I decided to move to another spot in the river, I couldn't move my feet. I tried lifting one leg and then the other, but both feet felt encased in cement, and nothing I tried seemed to work. I was stuck and stuck good.

The more I tried to extract my feet, the more I sank. Finally, in desperation I hit upon the idea of lifting my feet out of the waders, then pulling the waders out of the mud. If I hadn't thought of taking my feet out of the boots first, I might still be stuck there!

You've probably experienced being stuck, but perhaps in different ways. You may be feeling stuck in your life now, wanting more but unable to move ahead. When you're stuck in the past, the rest of the world passes you by, and all you can do is wave. You're not in the flow and you're not being blessed.

I talk to many people whose feet are mired in the mud and debris of their past and present experiences. Perhaps you could add to the list below of ways I have seen people stuck. Can you identify with some of them?

• Being stuck is setting goals but putting off doing anything to make them a reality.

• Being stuck is wanting everything to be perfect before taking a step.

• Being stuck is making a promise to yourself, to God, or someone else and not keeping it.

• Being stuck is not taking the steps you need to take to keep yourself from physical or emotional harm—or perhaps continuing to be a victim.

• Being stuck is waiting until things become so unbearable that you just can't take it anymore.

• Being stuck is allowing the fear of failure, disappointment, or change to keep you from taking the risk to change. Sometimes we don't take God at His word, because He doesn't come through the way we expect.

• Being stuck is the inability to see various alternatives that do exist.

• Being stuck is feeling helpless, frustrated, worthless, and hopeless.

• Being stuck is seeing life through a negative filter and expecting the worst from situations and people.

• Being stuck is underestimating the potential that God has given to you.

• Being stuck can be minimizing your situation, conditions, or problems—in other words, denial.

• Becoming and remaining stuck is a detour from blessing that may end up becoming a permanent route for the rest of your life. It bypasses all that God has for us. Regrets do this to us.[2]

The Blessing Robbers

Have you ever felt that life would be a lot easier if only those wounds and negative experiences from the past didn't keep interfering? Have you ever felt that way when you wake up in the morning? You just can't get going? I hear people say, "I really want to move ahead with my life. I'm committed to it, but it's so hard to get going."

I understand that. Sometimes hurts, issues from the past, or fear of the future slow us down. You have to keep trying and expending so much effort before you finally start moving ahead. Excess emotional baggage can bog you down rob you of blessing.

As a counselor for more than 25 years, I have talked with hundreds of people who are struggling with the effects of their past. Some of them are able to break free and move forward with their lives. Some cannot. Some struggle so hard just to make a slight bit of progress. Many are depressed because of what happened to them or because so many years were wasted before they finally came for counseling.

I've found that people deal with their emotional baggage in several inappropriate ways. Many of them are riddled with *regret over missed opportunities*. I often hear people say things like, "If only I had..." and "Oh, how I regret..." Another way we live our lives in the past is described by Jack Hayford as "the remembrance of reversals." It's similar to regrets except this time the focus is what might have been "if only that hadn't happened" and "if only I could have done it differently." Sometimes to expedite the process of growth and change, I ask counselees to make me a list of all of their "if only's" and regrets so we can tackle each of them and eventually put them to rest.

But many of the regrets I hear about are vain regrets. Whether we regret what was done to us by others or what we have done to others (sins), looking back to the past only cripples the blessings of the present and detours us from entering the future. I'm not saying that we should never regret the past. There is a place for this—once! And then we must begin moving in a new direction.

We all have baggage and personal failures from the past. The past is past, and the events in that time frame can never be changed. But the effects can.

John was a middle-aged man who had been in counseling for some time. He had experienced a number of difficulties growing up, and the effects had stayed with him. From time to time his unresolved problems from the past erupted and disrupted his family and work life. In counseling he tended to rehearse over and over what had happened to him and his poor choices at a younger age. The best way to put it is that he was bemoaning the past.

"John," I said, "it sounds like you really regret what has happened in the past. It also sounds like you feel that some of your life has been wasted because of the past. If that is so, wouldn't it be best now to focus your time and energy on moving on from what happened by making your present life different? I know the past can't be changed, but the present and future can.

"John, because you're a Christian and you don't have to live your life by yourself, why not let God restore those lost years by what He can do and help you do in the present? God is asking you to give Him the past and rejoice in who you are right at this moment because of Him. I think He has some surprises in store for you. What about it, John?"

What about you? You can get unstuck from the quicksand of past hurts by choosing to let God work in your life today.

Another dangerous tactic we use in handling the past is *recrimination*. We attempt to make others atone for what they did to us in the painful past. Blame and recrimination bring us to resentment, which leads to a lack of forgiveness, and we end up with a festering memory.

Another common response to the past is *renunciation*: We promise to change and do things differently. Past behaviors and attitudes are simply renounced, but they are not confronted and cleansed. Dr. Lloyd Ogilvie puts this so well when we says, "We try to close the door on what has been, but all we do is suppress the dragons of memory. Every so often they rap persistently and want to come out into our consciousness for a dress rehearsal in preparation for a rerun in a new situation or circumstance. Renunciation of our memories sounds so very pious. The only thing wrong with it is that it doesn't work."[3]

Instead of dragging along the unnecessary baggage of regret, blame, and renunciation, have you ever tried rejoicing over the past? That may sound strange, but rejoicing eventually brings release. Rejoicing over the past doesn't mean that you deny the hurtful incidents or the pain they brought you. Rather you come to the place where you no longer ask "why?" but "how?": How can I learn from what happened to me and be a different person because of it?

Live in the Present, Look to the Future

Some individuals are what I call "yesterday people," some are "today people," and others are "tomorrow people." Which are you? Yesterday people are those who have allowed the events of the past to dictate the parameters of their life today. They are also so preoccupied with the past that they are blind to the blessings of today.

If the past is invading your present, you already know it. You don't need anyone to tell you about it. You probably want to know, "What do I do about it?" Let's look at some answers to that question.

One of my favorite Old Testament characters is Joshua. The book of Joshua starts out in a very interesting manner. God is speaking, and He says to Joshua, "Moses my servant is dead" (1:2). Joshua knew that, of course. But perhaps he was too concerned about living in the shadow of his predecessor, so God reminded him of Moses' death to spur him to move on. Sometimes we need similar encouragement to stop being yesterday people and become today and tomorrow people. Jack Hayford describes it:

> Predecessors, plain people such as our parents, teachers or friends (even those disposed to our best interest) can cast shadows over our tomorrows. They may have set boundaries on our lives, limiting our view of ourselves or our potential. Or they may have been confined by boundaries of their own which found exact or mirrored images in us. But in either case, our predecessors often shape us, leaving an imprint which may be the source of our own present frustration.

How can we deal with this?

First, though God wants to free us unto tomorrow, He won't allow us to blame yesterday. Notice carefully how the Lord in saying "Moses is dead" makes no negative comment about Moses. Neither will He allow us to cast blame on anything or anybody who seems to restrict our tomorrows.[4]

The past is over (and the effects of the past can be taken care of as well), and it's time to become a today and tomorrow person. God's message to Joshua continued, "Now then, you and all these people, get ready to cross the Jordan River into the land I am about to give to them—to the Israelites" (v. 2). And then three times God made a statement to Joshua that He is also making to each of us: "Be strong and courageous."

The first time God said it, He told Joshua that He was giving the Israelites the land He had promised them (v. 6). Perhaps that's what will help us in our quest for growth and blessing: to remember that God keeps His promises. We can depend on Him. He comes through. When you look at the promises of His Word, remember that they have been given to us by God. You can count on them.

The second time God said, "Be strong and very courageous," He was telling Joshua to stick with Him. Don't turn aside. The verse actually says, "Be careful to obey all the law my servant Moses gave you; do not turn from it to the right or to the left, that you may be successful wherever you go" (v. 7). God is faithful, and He wants us to be faithful as well. Don't give up or quit on Him.

Perhaps the bottom line here is obedience. That's a difficult word for independent Americans. We like to be our own person. But it's interesting that one of the main catchall terms that characterizes people in our country today is co-dependency! We want to be independent, and yet end up being dependent on the wrong kind of person or situation. Dependency is all right when it's placed on God.

The next verse is a command to Joshua, and it really is what I'm hoping you'll see: "Do not let this Book of the Law depart from your mouth; meditate on it day and night, so that you may be careful to do everything written in it. Then you will be prosperous and successful" (v. 8).

There it is. Base your life on God's Word and discover the difference. It sounds like an ad comparing Coca-Cola and Pepsi, doesn't it? Taste and compare the difference between doing things your way and God's way. But what a difference!

People today want success. God wants us to be successful also, but it is His criteria we're to follow. We must integrate God's Word into our lives so it refines our beliefs, attitudes, and behavior. Again, I like the way Jack Hayford puts it: "God's Word gives much instruction for daily living, and the precepts and principles He gives aren't without good reason. While God didn't give life's laws so we could earn a way to heaven, He's provided them to make life work and to avoid a lot of hellishness!"[5]

The last time God said to Joshua, "Be strong and courageous," He also said, "Do not be terrified; do not be discouraged, for the Lord your God will be with you wherever you go" (v. 9). How are we to be strong? By laying hold of God's promises, laying hold of His patterns for life, and laying hold of Him![6]

Bankrupt by the Past

I heard an interesting story about a large corporation. The owner called together the district managers and explained to them that he needed their assistance in a very important program, because he was going to be unavailable for a period of time. The company needed to increase its income while he was gone, and it was up to the district managers to do it. Each manager would be given the responsibility for a sum of money, and it was up to each one to invest the funds wisely in order to generate additional income for the company. They could purchase stock futures, real estate, short term CDs, or whatever they could find. But they must use the funds distributed to them to make money.

A few months later the owner returned and once again called a meeting of these same managers. He asked for a report from each of them. All but one of them had doubled the money he had been assigned. But the last one made absolutely nothing. The owner was aghast. He just couldn't believe it. Had the delinquent district manager just put his money in the bank, he could have generated at least 5-6 percent interest in a standard savings account.

"Why didn't you do something with the money I gave you?" the owner asked.

The man replied, "I was afraid. I was afraid to take the risk and try."

This is an old story, of course, brought up to date. It was told by Jesus in Matthew 25:14-30. Jesus said that the servant who just sat on his money would have it taken from him. He lost it all.

There are people like this in our world. They have something to offer. They have abilities and gifts. They have resources and undeveloped or untapped potential. But because they live in the past, nothing is ever done with it. Yesterday people forfeit the blessings of the present and the future by wallowing in the past. Not only is the blessing of life lost, but in time the potential also diminishes and is lost.

No matter how much or how little we have, God asks us to do something with it and move on in life. If we don't, we live in a self-created prison. We were not meant to be prisoners. Jesus came to set the captives free. He opens the gates wide and says, "The choice is yours. Come with Me and be free. Begin living as a free person and be blessed."

"How can I cut loose from the past and walk in the blessings of today and tomorrow?" you ask. The next chapter provides some more detailed steps.

❦ *P R A Y E R* ❦

Dear Lord,

For too long I have lived more in the past than in the blessings of the future. I need help in identifying the baggage that is no longer essential in my life.

Thank You for being willing to take my regrets and banish them forever.

Show me the areas in which I need to move on in life, and instill within me the strength and courage You gave to Joshua and have promised to me.

Lord, I want to be a today and tomorrow person for You. I will look to the future for what You have for me. Thank You for choosing me for blessing.

In Jesus' name. Amen.

CHAPTER SIX

*Let Go
of the Past—
It's Possible!*

I f you take a glass jar, punch some air holes in the lid, and put several flies inside the jar, they will fly around and around desperately trying to find a way out of their prison. If the lid has been on for some time, the result is fascinating: When you take it off, the flies stay in the jar. That's right, they won't try to get away. The opening is clear, and all they have to do is fly up and out. But they won't. They will circle in the same pattern inside the jar. When they get close to the opening, they fly back down again. They continue to reenact their pattern of frustration and imprisonnt even though they are only inches from being free.

People are no different. We also fly around in the painful ruts of the past. And even when the lid is off and the possibility of being set free is before us, we often remain.[1]

What are the steps involved in cutting loose from the past and enjoying the blessings of today and tomorrow? Let's carefully examine them.

Identify the Problem

The first step in releasing the past is to become aware of the residue that still exists. Identify from your past those things that still bother you, affect you, influence you, or hinder you. It could be a person, event, experience, or erroneous belief. Take time to reflect on these issues.

Now select one issue you would like to change and clearly identify it below. It could be a feeling of bitterness, hurt, rejection, or fear that has lingered from the past. It could be the hurtful way you and a relative interact in person or on the phone. It could be a feeling you have about yourself that stems from your past or present relationship with a person or even an organization such as a church. It could be your damaging negative beliefs about yourself. After dealing with this issue, take the same approach with subsequent issues, isolating them, identifying them, and dealing with them one by one.

It will also be helpful for you to identify the reasons why you want to work through these issues and change their impact on your life. Thoughtfully list these reasons in the space provided by completing the statement: "I want to change because..."

Issue: _____
I want to change because...

Issue: _____
I want to change because...

Issue: _____
I want to change because...

For some of you, the intensity of the past event may have caused you to deny or suppress some of your memories of what happened. This sometimes occurs because you don't want to admit the severity of what took place. But when you repress and block out painful experiences and feelings, you often block out the good experiences also. Invite the Holy Spirit to reveal those issues, events, memories, or people you need to deal with.

Expose Your False Hidden Beliefs

The second step in cutting the line to your past is to identify and expose false hidden beliefs. What false ideas from your past have caused you to grow up believing certain wrong things about yourself? Some of the beliefs you carry today have been blown way out of proportion. They're irrational. That can happen to any of us. For example, the false belief that all men are abusive prevents some women from dating or befriending any men. Some men feel that all women live solely on their feelings, because that's the way these men perceived their mothers and sisters. These false beliefs must be exposed and corrected before you can move on in your life.

Your hidden beliefs are like invisible reins attached to you and held by some hurtful issue in your past. Many of the decisions in your life were probably made in response to the way others directly or indirectly pulled on the reins to control you. I've seen this happen in my counselees' relationships with their parents, siblings, aunts and uncles, friends, teachers, and ministers. Today you either move toward or away from people or events because of what you learned from the experiences of the past.

In order to uncover some of your false beliefs, answer the following questions regarding each issue or problem from your past:

1. As you were growing up, what did you do to handle the problem?

2. What did you believe you must stop doing or give up in order to keep the same situation from repeating itself?

3. What did you believe you had to become or do in order to feel secure and protected? Were these beliefs tied

75

into gaining the love and acceptance of any significant person?

4. What types of fears or concerns did you develop about other people and situations that were tied into your relationship with your past?

Some people have discovered that they made decisions based on false beliefs that caused them to be clinging, possessive, or overcautious in their relationships, to avoid risks at all costs, to second-guess themselves, or to not trust themselves. An important question you must answer is, "What self-limiting decisions did I make years ago that may have affected my life in the present?"[2]

You may falsely believe that what happened in your past was so devastating and painful that you will be hindered by it for the rest of your life. You may have been emotionally rejected for years or physically or sexually abused. You may feel that the future is as bleak as your past. But that belief is false. There *is* hope. Recovery *is* possible. Change in feelings, attitudes, and beliefs *can* occur. Coping isn't your *only* choice.

In cases where wounds from the past are deep and severe, it may take years to work through the issues. In others where the hurt is not as severe, healing can occur in a much shorter amount of time.

Release Your Past

The third step to cutting the line to your past is to let yourself and any significant people who hurt you off the hook. In order to take this step you must believe that it is possible to leave past hurts behind. You can't use half-hearted phrases like, "Well, I'll try" or "I'll do it if..." You must make a determined commitment to change and move forward confidently on that commitment. Let Jesus Christ take charge of your life and give you the direction and strength you need.

As you think about taking this step, your mind may be flooded with a number of objections. These thoughts usually come from a sense of powerlessness to change your situation. You may hear yourself complaining:

• I've had these feelings for such a long time. I can't change them.

• I'll always be this way.

• I've tried all that I know to do, but nothing works.

• I've tried for so long, and I'm tired. It's not worth the effort.

Counteract these objections by committing yourself to practice consistently the suggestions in this book for six months. Then you can decide if your inner statements are true or not. Give yourself a trial period for applying some new approaches to your relationships. Remember: You *can* change your attitudes, beliefs, responses, and feelings whether or not the other person changes.

If you are hesitant to move forward because you feel overwhelmed by the power your past has over you, consider this: By failing to deal with your past, you are giving more power to whatever it was that happened. "That's an unfair statement," you may say. But how long has your past already controlled you? If you have spent several years of your adult life allowing yourself to be dominated by the past, you have supplied some of the power that allowed it to happen.

Breaking free from the past involves a process of recovery. What is recovery? It is being able to reflect on your past and how it contributed to your identity, both positive and negative, without allowing the negative to control your present life. Recovery is finding new meaning in your present life by ridding yourself of the contamination of the past. It means claiming your circumstances instead of letting your circumstances claim you.[3]

Let Yourself Off the Hook

If you are burdened down with blame and guilt over the past, remember: Blaming yourself is like playing with a loaded gun. You will eventually get hurt. When you blame yourself for things over which you had no control, you may also take out your feelings on anyone who happens to get in your way.

Much of the guilt and blame you feel may be tied to your behavior as a child in response to whatever happened. Be aware that you were not responsible for what happened to you as a young child. You didn't have either the coping mechanisms or the defenses to make the right responses. You can see this today in the way a child handles a crisis. In a moment of fear, a six-year-old may revert to behaving like a three-year-old because that's the only way she knows how to respond to fear. She's not at fault for responding like a three-year-old. She just hasn't accumulated the life experiences to develop a repertoire of appropriate responses. Let yourself off the hook for the inappropriate ways you handled your problems when you were a child. You are not to blame.

You may also need to experience forgiveness for adult behaviors you are responsible for in your relationship with others. Let me remind you of an important passage from the Word of God: "If we walk in the light as He Himself is in the light, we have fellowship with one another, and the blood of Jesus His Son cleanses us from all sin.... If we confess our sins, He is faithful and righteous to forgive us our sins and to cleanse us from all unrighteousness" (1 John 1:7,9, NASB).

If God has forgiven your sins, who are you to contradict Him? Take God's perspective on your failures and receive His forgiveness.

In order to help you discover areas where you need to receive forgiveness, take a few moments to answer the following questions.

1. List some of the things you feel badly about from your childhood.

2. For each behavior, list at least two reasons why you think you did it.

3. Do you feel personally responsible for each of these behaviors? Why or why not?

4. Complete this statement: I feel I need forgiveness for...

5. Complete this statement: I accept the forgiveness of Jesus Christ for the following things I did as a child:

6. What have you done as an adult that is a direct result of your experiences as a child?

7. For each behavior, list at least two reasons why you think you did it.

8. For which of these behaviors do you feel personally responsible?

9. Complete this statement: I feel I need forgiveness for...

10. Complete this statement: I accept the forgiveness of Jesus Christ for the following things I did as an adult.[4]

This Is Your Life

People feel unblessed for many different reasons. Some are working through traumas from the past. Some are working through simple misbeliefs they were taught in the past. Others are working through a major loss which they experienced during the past year. In most cases it is helpful for the person to put everything into perspective by picturing their life experiences or their losses on paper in the form of a time-line chart. I ask them to identify both good or positive experiences throughout their life as well as negative or hurtful experiences. Too often we remember and concentrate only on the negative memories.

You may find it helpful to construct a time-line for your own life. You can use the space on the following page which I've labeled for you. Above the line list the negative incidents from your life which you feel are still affecting you in the present. These are the hurts, upsets, disappointments, or even traumas that may have occurred in the past.

One man listed three broken engagements during ages 17-26. He is single at 35 and hesitant to ask anyone to marry him. But as he filled in the bottom portion of the chart, which contains the positive life experiences, he discovered that he had a few healthy relationships with women too, several of whom asked him to marry them! Listing these experiences on the time-line helped him put everything in perspective.

One person traced the seeds of his 12-year depression to two parental rejections during his teens. One was when they stopped attending his Little League games, and the other was that they showed little or no interest in his activities in high school. But on the positive side, he also saw that his parents' intention was not to reject him. They just wanted to give him as much independence as possible by staying out of his way. He saw their uninvolvement as disinterest. Misunderstandings like this happen when there is insufficient communication.

As you reflect on your life and fill in the chart, try to identify the year in which each event happened. Use a

Life Event Chart

Negative Events

Birth ————————————————— Present

Positive Events

vertical line intersecting the horizontal line to place each event.

Now look at your time-line and complete the following exercises.

1. Write a paragraph or two describing each incident on the chart, including the feelings you experienced when it occurred and your feelings now. Indicate how the event is still affecting your life at the present time.

2. Using the steps to releasing the past presented earlier in this chapter, describe in writing how you will break free from each incident's hold on you.

3. Describe how you will relinquish your feelings about each event.

I'm sure everyone has some memories they would like to purge from their mind. Some have more than others. Have you experienced God's grace and forgiveness for your past experiences and memories? I've talked to people who have invited the Holy Spirit to take the hurt and pain away from those memories. It is possible to see those memories change from being emotional memories to harmless historical memories. Emotional memories carry the hurt, pain, remorse, and perhaps resentment with them. Historical memories are just that: an event of history. "Yes, it happened," you say, "but I can remember it now without the pain. And since it is only a fact of my history, I am going on with my life and creating healthy and positive memories which will influence my life and help me enjoy God's blessing."

Once you have dealt with the past, you must turn your focus to embracing a positive vision for the future. In the next chapter, we'll learn how.

❧ P R A Y E R ❧

Dear Lord,

Please focus my attention on any area of my life where I am stuck in the past and unaware of it. I want my ruts to be too uncomfortable for me to stay in any longer.

Help me to break the bondage of failures and disappointments and their self-imposed limitations. I don't want to remember my reversals, but I do want to remember the ways You have worked in my life.

May my thoughts and actions be based upon directives from Your Word. I want to bring my limiting beliefs and enslavements to You to be cast out of my life.

In Jesus' name. Amen.

Part Three:

MOVING TOWARD A BLESSED FUTURE

CHAPTER SEVEN

Catching
a Vision
for Blessing

He sat with hands extended, crying out for handouts. That's the only way he could let others know he needed something from them. Most people never even looked his way. They had seen beggars like him before. Oh, they heard him all right. But even when some people did swing out of their path to drop a morsel of food or a small coin in his hand, it was never enough. He kept his hands out, and he kept crying out.

He was dirty, dusty.

His hair was matted.

He was a reject from society.

He was Bartimaeus, and he was blind. He could only "see" with his ears and his hands. He didn't know what you and I know about the wonder of seeing. How can you explain a soft, white, billowy cloud to a blind man? How can you explain the vivid lavender streaks of a sunset to the sightless? How do you put into words the various hues of green in a field or forest? But he wanted to see it all. He wanted to see people and sunsets and animals. He wanted to see life.

One day the air around him swirled heavy with dirt and dust. A large crowd was passing by, and Bartimaeus heard them. He asked what all the commotion was about.

He was told that the healer was coming, the man Jesus. Bartimaeus had heard of Jesus. He had even heard the rumor that Jesus was the one Isaiah talked about: "A light for the Gentiles, to open eyes that are blind, to free captives from prison and to release from the dungeon those who sit in darkness" (Isaiah 42:6-7).

Without hesitating, he cried out to Jesus. His request was simple, and he was persistent. People told him to be quiet, but he wouldn't stop crying out. He was consumed with his desire. This was his only chance.

Suddenly Bartimaeus felt hands lifting him up from the dirt and helping him walk toward Jesus. Once again Jesus asked a question, the answer to which He already knew. But that was His way much of the time, wasn't it? Everyone knew what the man wanted. But there was a reason for the question, a lesson for the others to see.

How did Jesus ask the question?

With a sigh?

With boldness?

With hesitation?

Who knows? What matters is that He asked the man, "What do you want me to do?" And very simply the desire that burned within the blind man for years was stated: "I want to see!" Bartimaeus was saying:

> I want out of the dungeon, out of the darkness. I want out of the shackles of these blind eyes. I want out of the prison. I want to be free. "I want to see!"

> I want to get off of the roadside. I want to walk the streets of Jericho without running into its walls. I want to look in the shops. I want to find my way to the synagogue. "I want to see!"

> I want to use my hands for something besides feeling my way in the dark. I want to make things. I want to fix my own meals. I want to read. "I want to see!"

I want to look into the eyes of a friend. I want to wave at someone across the way. I want to smile at children and pat their heads and wish them well.... I want to love. I want to laugh. I want to live. "I want to see!"[1]

And he did see (see Luke 18:35-43). He could finally experience what we take for granted. Can you imagine the discoveries and delights of each moment after he could see? Do you think he ever took his newfound treasure for granted?

Dreams and Vision Release Blessing

Have you ever cried out with the fervor Bartimaeus displayed? Have you asked Jesus for sight?

New sight?

A new vision?

What would happen if you let God expand your vision for rest of your life?

When we're stuck in the past for any length of time, our vision becomes defective. When we focus on the hurts and failures of yesterday, we become blind to the blessings of today and tomorrow. If we turned our eyes toward the future we could see where we want to go. Better yet, we could see where God would like to lead us. And if we did that, perhaps we would have a vision for the future. Visions open up the doorway to blessing.

Have you ever had a dream? No, I don't mean the dreams we all have while asleep, but a conscious dream, a heart's desire. You longed for something or someone with an element of hope, thinking that perhaps, just perhaps, your longing would be realized.

Some people have been through such pain and disruption they never learn how to dream. It's the last thing on their mind. And yet we need to dream, for it is out of dreams that lives and history are changed and blessings are realized.

91

Sometimes dreamers are scoffed at. Joseph was a dreamer and was subject to ridicule from his brothers (see Genesis 37). Sometimes dreams fade if we receive too much negative reaction. Sometimes we start to disbelieve our own dreams and become content to remain right where we are.

But dreams can also be contagious. Do you remember the dream of the man that day in 1963 who stood in front of thousands of people and cried out again and again, "I have a dream"? His dream was for justice and equality for black people. He never gave up on his dream, and the dream of Martin Luther King, Jr. is now part of mainstream American consciousness. Dr. David Seamands, who heard Dr. King cry out his dream that day, says simply, "That day I learned the awesome power of an awe-inspiring dream, and I returned home lifted and encouraged."[2]

The prophet said it for us: "Your old men will dream dreams, your young men will see visions" (Joel 2:28). When you have vision, you may find yourself battling upstream, but you'll experience God's blessing and His presence as you cooperate with His work in your life. When you see things as they could be, you won't let the odds overwhelm you. When you see things as they could be, you'll recognize obstacles, but you won't dwell on them. When you see things as they could be, you'll experience today and anticipate tomorrow.

Do you know what vision is? Here's what Chuck Swindoll says:

 Vision is the ability to see God's presence, to perceive God's power, to focus on God's plan in spite of the obstacles....Vision is the ability to see above and beyond the majority. Vision is perception—reading the presence and power of God into one's circumstances. I sometimes think of vision as looking at life through the lens of God's eyes, seeing situations as He sees them. Too often we see things not as they are, but as we are. Think about that. Vision has to do with looking at life with a divine perspective, reading the scene with God in clear focus.

Whoever wants to live differently in "the system" must correct his or her vision.[3]

What happens as you begin to dream with God? How will it impact your life? Your attitude is fitted with a new lens. Your new "glasses" are amazing. When you wear them you see the possibilities rather than the problems. Your thought life and vocabulary undergo a change. "I can't" and "It won't work" are now foreign phrases. You can now say, "If God is for me, who can be against me? With His help, I *can*... , I *will*...." You become optimistic and hopeful. You remember whose child you are, who has adopted you, and who is guiding and empowering your life.

When you have vision, you begin to think of the impossible as possible. The late Dr. Henrietta Mears, founder of Gospel Light Publications and Forest Home Christian Conference Center, once said, "There is no magic in small plans. When I consider my ministry, I think of the world. Anything less than that would not be worthy of Christ nor His will for my life."

Do you remember when you were in school reading the exploits of the pioneers in this country? Perhaps you watched programs about them on television or in some of the older movies. Pioneers were people with a sense of adventure. Most of them could have continued to live right where they were before they branched out on their adventure. But they weren't content. They believed there was something better out there. Somewhere there was greater potential, more freedom, more to life than staying where they were.

I remember reading about some of the exploits of famous pioneers and thinking, "Wouldn't it have been great to live during that time so I could be a pioneer? We don't have that opportunity today." Right? Wrong. Pioneering still occurs today, but it just has a different format. We still have people pioneering in remote places like the Yukon and Alaska. We have people pioneering with new businesses, ideas, and inventions. We have people willing to move beyond their comfort zones to fulfill dreams and conquer new territory.

Every Christian is called to be a pioneer. We are called to be different, to act in a new way, to think in a new way, to treat other people in a new way, and to see life through new lenses. Christians are transformational people. We are called to change. If we are not moving forward and changing, we are stagnating—and stagnant ponds stink!

Dreams and Vision Draw Us Forward

Our God-inspired dreams and vision should be like a magnet that draws us out of the past and into the blessings of the future. I thought of this recently while watching the popular film, *Dances with Wolves*. I was greatly intrigued with the animal scenes. During the stampede scene there were hundreds of buffalo thundering across the plain. At one point a buffalo appeared to be charging directly at an Indian boy. I wondered, "How did the film makers get that buffalo to do what they wanted?"

I later discovered in a magazine article that a great deal of time had been invested in the scene with that one buffalo. In order to get the buffalo to cooperate, they conditioned it by feeding it Oreo cookies. It wasn't long before the animal would practically jump through a hoop to get to those round, chocolate, cream-filled cookies. So for the stampede scene they placed a pile of Oreos next to the Indian boy (and out of sight of the camera), and the cookies drew the buffalo in the right direction just like a powerful magnet.

What would your life be like today, right at this moment, if you had your vision in mind and were thinking and responding as if that vision were a reality? What would your future as a child of God be like if you allowed your scripturally based vision for you life to draw you forward?

One of the current figures in the field of effective management and character development is Stephen Covey. He has challenged many leaders with the basic principles of his program. He encourages leaders to begin each day with a mental picture of the end of their life as the criteria for everything they choose to do each day.

For many people, this idea is revolutionary. But for the Christian, it shouldn't be. This is our calling when we invite Jesus Christ into our lives. Some people call it "having a goal." But I think it is part of the vision we need that allows us to experience God's blessing as we proceed through life.

Think of it this way: Would you act any differently today if you first considered what you eventually want to happen in your life? Do you have a clear picture of your destination? Do you really know where you are going with your life? Do you keep your picture for your life clearly in mind?

I've been in seminars where the speaker asked us to write down what we want people to say about us after we die. Perhaps that is a disturbing thought, and yet when you think about it, it makes sense. If we want certain things to be expressed about us, what are we doing now to make that a reality? Is the way we are living our lives now consistent with those statements?

Perhaps another way of saying this is, "Do you have a blueprint for your life that you are following?" You might ask, "Now where in the world would I ever get a blueprint for my life?" We already have one in the Word of God. The Bible is God's plan book for building our lives on His blessing.

You have probably already created visions for your life without realizing it. You may have called them goals or objectives, but some of them were visions, real dreams. You pictured something you wanted to occur in the future, and you began moving toward making it a reality.

Often in counseling I work with husbands and wives who don't feel that they love their partners. Fortunately, some of them want to develop their love, but they are stumped as to how to make that happen. The suggestion I give time and time again is, "Let's imagine together what it would be like if you did love your partner. Describe how you would feel about him, how you would treat him, think about him, support him, and defend him before others." And so we discuss this for a while.

Then I usually say, "I would like you to write out in detail this vision you have created for loving your partner and read it over several times a day. I would like you to pray about each facet of this vision, and ask God to make this love come alive within you. And then I want you to behave toward your partner as though you actually did love him or her. Do this for the next month. Let's see what happens."

Do I need to spell out for you what often happens? That vision becomes a reality.

Having a vision means that you have an idea where you are going before you start out on the trip. And you don't sit there and simply hope that your vision finds you. The Word of God often tells us what we need to do for progress to occur. Like Bartimaeus, we need to step out in faith, "see" the unseen possibilities, grasp them daily through prayer and action, and realize the blessings.

Plotting the Future

How do you determine the vision for your life? It will come from asking God to help you discover the possibilities. It will come from spending time in His Word discovering what He wants for you personally. That's where the blessings begin.

You're about to embark on a journey of choice and change. But for any journey you have to consider what you will take with you and where you want to go. Spend time in prayer asking God to renew your mind, sharpen your insight, and activate your motivation. Fasten your hope on this passage: "'For I know the plans I have for you,' declares the Lord, 'plans to prosper you and not to harm you, plans to give you hope and a future'" (Jeremiah 29:11).

In order to help you begin to grasp your vision, let me ask you some blunt and direct questions. To help you personalize what you're learning, write your answers right here in the book. Your answers are for your eyes only.

1. How old are you?

2. How long do you want to live? Please respond with a specific number of years rather than saying, "That's in the Lord's hands" or "I have nothing to do with it." Yes, it's in the Lord's hands, but you do have something to do with it.

3. How long do you plan to live? Whether you realize it or not, you are already involved in determining how long you will live. The way you treat your body with regard to food, drink, alcohol, tobacco, rest, stress, worry, anger impacts your plan for longevity.

Let's take what you've written and combine it with what you've experienced in your life up to this time using the time-line on the next page. At the left end of the line, place the year of your birth and put an X above it. At the

97

X
——
1937

X
——
1992

X
——
2037

right end of the line, place the year that represents how long you want to live or plan to live with an X above it. Then place the current year at the appropriate place on the line with an X above it. Finally, draw 10 vertical lines between the year of your birth and today.

Reflect back on your life and identify what you would consider God's blessings. Remember: A blessing is the assurance that you belong to God and the transmission or endowment of the power of His goodness or favor in your life. Now, for each of the vertical lines on your chart, write down one of the blessings you recall.

Look at the space on the chart representing the years between today and the end of your life. Answer the following questions for this time period:

1. What is your vision for your relationship with God?

2. What is your vision for incorporating God's Word into your life?

3. What blessings from God you would like to experience?

4. In what way do you want to be a blessing to others? to your spouse? to your children?

5. What new experiences do you want for your life? in your work?

6. What is your vision for your thought life? your emotional life?

7. What is your vision for the next year of your life? the next five years? for what will be said about you at the end of your life?

Now write a letter to God on your sheet of paper telling Him about the next year of your life. (A letter to God is very much like a prayer. Some people actually pray better by writing their thoughts in letter form.) Tell Him about your vision for your life, what you anticipate, what risks you are going to take, and what you would like to accomplish. Tell Him what blessings you are looking forward to, and ask Him what steps you need to take for these blessings to occur.

Following through with these exercises doesn't automatically mean that your life will be flooded with blessing. But you will be taking some positive steps away from your confining past and in the direction of the blessings God wants to pour out to you in the days ahead. Does moving ahead sound risky to you? Does the possibility of change in your life trigger an anxious response in the pit of your stomach? Read on. The chapters that follow will prepare you to deal with the risks and changes involved in pursuing God's blessing.

🍎 P R A Y E R 🍎

Dear Lord,

Often I sit with my hands outstretched just waiting for You to bless me. I'm not much different from Bartimaeus. I have my own dungeons of blindness even when my eyes are wide open.

Help me see the blessings I have already received that I tend to overlook.

Lord, I want to be a person of vision. Help me discover and fashion the dream You would have me pursue. May my thoughts and ways be Your thoughts and ways.

Take my fears, even though I have been accustomed to living with them each day. Break their blinding power so I can live a life of freedom in You and capture the visions You have for me.

In Jesus' name. Amen.

CHAPTER EIGHT

The Risk of Being Blessed

A number of years ago there was a series on television called The Waltons. It was one of my all-time favorite shows, and we watched practically every episode together as a family.

One night on The Waltons there was a very dramatic, poignant scene between the husband and wife. The seven-minute interaction was a classic model of a difficult yet healthy and positive communication exchange. At that time I was involved in conducting marriage enrichment seminars and couples classes, and I made the remark, "What a tremendous scene. I sure wish I could show it at my seminars."

My daughter Sheryl, who was in her early teens, said, "Why don't you call them and ask them if you can use it?"

I must have looked at her with an expression that communicated, "Oh, come on, Sheryl. They would never let me use that film clip. TV networks just don't do that kind of thing." And I'm sure I said something to that effect. At the moment I was blinded to the possibilities by the risk of asking and being rejected. Sheryl's last comment was, "Well, you could at least try."

The next day, after reflecting on what she said, I called the TV station. I thought, "What do I have to lose? All they can do is refuse me." A month later, after two letters to the network, I held in my hand a 16mm print of that seven-minute scene. The letter (which floored me) read, "Here is the print you requested. There is no charge. We receive requests all the time, but never fill them. We trust this will be of benefit to you as you work with couples." Was I ever surprised!

In the next few years that film clip was shown to thousands of people in my seminars, and it became a memorable and helpful experience for them. But it would never have happened had I not listened to the suggestion of my daughter. I had to take a risk. I had to change my thinking and behavior. A great risk resulted in a great blessing.

The Challenge of Change

As you look at your time line, your answers to the questions, and your letter to God in the last chapter, you probably realize that activating your vision will require some—perhaps many—concrete changes. When someone mentions the word "change" to you, is your response one of hope and anticipation or hesitation and fear? Some people approach change with a sense of eagerness, but not everyone does. Maybe you're among those who balk at the prospect of changing your approach to life.

Change is usually easier to talk about than to bring about because it means that things are going to be different, alterations are going to occur. Many people believe that change is just something that happens to them, something over which they have no control. They adapt to it because they have to or they are forced to, not because they choose to.

Even when change has a positive outcome, it can be uncomfortable and painful. We become comfortable with sameness and routine, even if it happens to be negative or destructive. Some people, especially men, hesitate about making a change in their marital or family relationships unless they experience a crisis. In fact, most people make the greatest changes in their lives when they experience a crisis. Why? Because they discover that what used to work for them no longer works! Thus they are forced to change. It's as if we have to experience the worst consequences before we change.

However, this is not always the case. We used to believe that alcoholics could not change until they suffered the worst consequences of their drinking. But now we know that they can change before that happens. Hitting bottom doesn't have to be our starting point for change. When you and I decide that we want our lives to be different, change can happen. The first step is making the choice to change.

Risky? Yes.

Threatening? Perhaps.

Will I feel out of control? You may, for a time at least.

Will my change challenge or threaten others? Probably.

Will change happen immediately? Probably not.

Will others help me in the process? Yes, if you select those who care for you and want the best for you.

Who else will help me? God.

Is there more potential for me if I choose to change than if I stay the way I am? Will I experience more of God's blessing in my life if I choose to change? Absolutely!

Risking a Choice

Choosing to change is risky. Are you a risk-taker? It's risky to be a risk-taker. I know. I've taken a few. It's unsettling. It's unnerving. It produces some anxiety, because we want to know the outcome of our choices in advance. There is a risk in seeking a new job. What if you are rejected, not just by one potential employer but by several? There is a risk in asking someone out on a date or asking someone to marry you. What if they say no? That would hurt. But think of the blessing you could miss by not trying, by not asking, by not taking the risk.

I remember the risk of climbing out on a four-inch ledge to creep around a cliff jutting out over the icy water of a high altitude lake. To add to the difficulty, I had to let go of one handhold to continue creeping along the ledge to reach the next handhold eight feet away. What if my foot slipped and I plunged 20 feet to the frigid water below? It was a risk. But I chose to take that risk to get to the inlet of the lake. It was worth it as we landed many brilliant golden trout for the next two hours.

I remember the risk of walking into a bank and asking for a loan of $2000. It doesn't sound like much, does it? But 20 years ago, when I was earning only $7000 a year, $2000 was a very large amount to me. And I was taking a risk. I intended to use the money to publish my own curriculum on marriage. I felt so strongly that this curriculum was needed so others could teach marriage enrichment classes in their churches. I felt God's leading coupled with my own convictions. But it still wasn't easy to take out that loan. Where was the assurance that others would buy these books? What if they didn't sell or other people didn't see the same benefit in them I did?

But I took the risk. The plan was approved. The manuals were printed. They sold, and the monies earned funded the start-up of Christian Marriage Enrichment, which is now a nationwide ministry of training and producing curriculum for churches. It took a risk, but the blessings enjoyed by thousands of couples over the years have been well worth it.

You say you're not a risk-taker? Everyone is to one degree or another. Perhaps you've just never identified all the risks you've taken in your lifetime. Take a sheet of paper and list several things you once could not do but now are able to do. Begin with very simple items like driving a car. Keep adding to your list for a week. You will be amazed at what you discover. You have grown. You have accomplished much in your life. God has been at work in your life. And everything you learned to do involved a risk. Use this list as a reminder that you are indeed a risk-taker. As you continue to take risks for change and growth, you will discover that you are a blessed person!

When you take a risk you have to open your hand and loosen your hold on what is certain. You have to reach out for something that is a bit uncertain, but it's usually better than what you have at the present time. Tim Hansel, who is certainly a risk-taker, writes:

> Have you ever thought what your life would be like if you had never taken a risk? You probably would have never learned to walk, never moved away from home, never made a friend, and never really gone anywhere or done anything the least bit memorable. The truth is, we cannot grow without taking risks, without loosening our grip on the known and the certain, and taking a chance in reaching for a little bit more of life. Some people are content with mere routine, a revolving-door existence of waking up, eating breakfast, going to work, coming home, going to bed. But others seem infected with a rage to live. Their secret is that they are always beginning something new.[1]

To change and grow, you have to risk. To move ahead, you have to risk. To find what is worthwhile in life, you have to risk. To risk means giving up some security (even though some of what we call security is really false; it doesn't really give us what we think it does). The man at the Pool of Bethesda had to risk. He had to answer Jesus' question about wanting to be healed, which cut through all his excuses. Blind Bartimaeus had to risk. He raised a ruckus to attract the Master's attention. And their risks paid off in fantastic blessings.

Hesitation Leads to Frustration

Perhaps one of the best ways to identify the steps involved in any risk is with the example of passing another car on a two-lane highway. There is a 25-mile stretch of highway in the high desert area of Southern California that I travel once or twice a year. It's not my favorite stretch of road because of the limitation of the two lanes and the frequent dips in the road that tend to hide oncoming cars.

When I'm stuck behind a slow-plodding driver, I have the choice of staying behind him or looking for an opportunity to pass. When I think about passing, I must not only observe the slow vehicle I'm following but watch the road for oncoming traffic. Then I have to determine if there is enough highway between me and the approaching cars to allow me to pass.

These are the stages in taking the risk of passing on the highway: preparing adequately, making a commitment, then following through by pressing the accelerator to the floor, surging around the slow driver, and moving back into your lane. This process is successful for most people when they follow all the procedures. But it doesn't work for the driver who hesitates and vacillates when he pulls out into the other lane. Losing his nerve and not accelerating properly can lead to a tragic accident.

Similarly, when we risk and choose to change, we must be committed to follow through if we are to realize the blessings that change and growth promise.

I would rather choose to take a risk than be forced into taking one. Which would you prefer? If we postpone taking risks when they are needed, we may be forced to accept something we don't want or to take risks when we are least prepared for them.

Howard Hughes, one of the richest men of the 20th century, is a good example of what can happen when we risk—and when we refuse to take risks. Hughes greatly impacted the aircraft industry with bold risks for change, helping the U.S. maintain dominance in the sky during several wars. He helped establish the movie industry and influenced the entertainment industry. He gained tremendous power, and his power affected not only our country and society but the world.

Howard Hughes was a pioneer at risk-taking for a large part of his life. But then he changed. He redirected his energies to becoming a fanatic at protecting himself against risk. He created a virtual prison for himself in his attempt to insulate himself from decisions, people, germs, or anything else he perceived to be a risk. He was worth billions, but he chose to live in a hotel room and vegetate until he died. He ended up a fearful old man who didn't trust anyone, a prisoner when he could have been free. When Howard Hughes stopped risking he stopped living.[2]

If we don't risk, our world grows smaller. It shrinks. We become comfortable with sameness and stagnation. We invest our energy in keeping life the way it is. We resist growth. We become reactors rather than making things happen. When we don't risk, we are the losers. When we don't risk, we risk missing the blessings God has for us.

The Red Light of Fear

The fear of risking is the fear of being hurt or laughed at, experiencing failure, being rejected, showing our imperfections, or somehow failing as a person. Somewhere along the path of life we decide, consciously or subconsciously, never to take a risk. Before long we become turtles tucked inside a shell, immobile and detached from life and blessing. Like the turtle, we only make progress when we stick our necks out by risking change.

Fear is a glaring red light on the highway of risk and change leading to blessing. Fear cripples. Fear disables. Fear clouds our vision. Fear shortens life. Fear cripples our relationships with others. Fear blocks our relationship with God. Fear keeps us from experiencing the blessings of God, because it short-circuits our choices and keeps us from change. You and I have freedom in Christ, yet we often choose to walk through life in a mobile prison of fear.

There are many ways fear blocks our choices and subsequent changes. Fear can talk you into limiting your vision, and consequently you do less than you are capable of. "What if I attempt too much and don't make it or it takes away from my time with other activities?" Fear can cause us to imagine the worst possible outcome of our efforts. Giving in to questions like these can restrict us.

Fear can limit the development of various alternatives and put the brakes on pursuing them. To protect ourselves from the disappointment that could occur if our efforts don't work out, we settle for less, and dreams and hope fade.

Fear has a warping effect. It warps our perceptions of our life and what we could do to move ahead in a positive way. Unchecked fears soon begin to destroy the reality of what might have been.[3]

Fear keeps us from saying, "I can...," "I will...," "I'm able..." as well as "God is able..."! Whenever you give in to your fears, they grow larger, become more real, and finally limit you from being the dreamer and visionary that will lead to change in your life.

Fear turns people into yesterday people. Their resistance keeps them from experiencing the blessings that God has for them. They are unable to focus their thinking and beliefs and move ahead.

If you fear making choices and ultimately changing, try this idea. Write down your fear, then ask three other people if they believe it's a realistic fear. If it is, spend five minutes a day committing it to God. List everything that could go wrong with your vision because of this fear. For every possible thing that could go wrong, list two things you could do to correct it. Finally, for every reason you have created to keep yourself from moving ahead, list two reasons why it actually *is* possible to move ahead.

The Green Light of Faith

As believers in Christ we are all risk-takers to some degree. We learn to live by faith. Faith is the green light within that keeps us pursuing our dreams and vision for blessing despite our fear of risk and change. The more faith we have, the more we become risk-takers. Dr. Lloyd Ogilvie talks about the risk-taking heroes of the Old Testament:

> Faith is risky. It isn't real faith without a risk. A willingness to risk was all that God asked of them. The greater the risk, the greater the power of faith given them. And those who dared to risk in attempting the impossible found the liberating truth that we all desperately need for life's awesome challenges. They discovered that the Creator and Sustainer of the universe is the Lord of the impossible![4]

Being a risk-taker doesn't mean we don't experience some fear, hesitation, or reservation. I can just imagine the inner response of Abraham when God said to him, "Abraham, I want you to leave your country, leave your relatives, leave your father's house, and move to a land which I will show you" (see Genesis 12:1). Abraham had never been to this new land. Probably no one else he knew had either. And then to leave the security of his family. What was God asking?

Abraham didn't have an auto club to call and request detailed directions. There were no Burger King restaurants on the way for food, no service stations for the camels, no place to stop and ask directions. This was a giant risk. All Abraham could go on was the promise of God. And His promises were really something. He said in Genesis 12:2-3: "I will make you into a great nation and I will bless you; I will make your name great, and you will be a blessing. I will bless those who bless you, and whoever curses you I will curse; and all peoples on earth will be blessed through you."

Abraham probably experienced moments of fear, and there may have been times en route when he was tempted to turn back to the security of his homeland. But he stuck his neck out, took the risk, followed through. And he was blessed.

God has also chosen you for blessing. Oh, He probably isn't calling you to leave your homeland and family and begin a new nation. That was Abraham's unique call. But God may be calling you to something just as risky and fear-producing for where you are in life today. As you have developed a vision, considered the changes that need to be made, and weighed the risks, have you discovered what your unique call is?

He many be calling you to take a risk to improve your marriage relationship.

He may be calling you to build a bridge of love between you and an estranged relative or friend.

He may be calling you to take on a new ministry at church, something you never dreamed you could do.

He may be calling you to take a stand for righteousness in your place of employment.

Only you know just what God is calling you to do to change and grow and find blessing. Will you respond in fear or in faith? It's your choice.

Is there a future? Yes, there is!

Is there a hopeful future? Yes, there is!

Let these words dwell within your heart and mind today and bless you:

In Christ I am free to live, free to be flexible, free to move, free to fail, free to succeed. I can confidently know that there are things I will do well and things that I will not be able to do at all. I don't have to try to prove to myself or to others that somehow I can be what I am not. God made me; God owns me.

And as I relax in Christ, I begin to see that there have always been people like me. This reinforces my certainty. I meet people in Scripture—people like Abraham, Moses, Stephen—who did not fully understand themselves or their purpose, but they knew that God understood them. They did not always feel strong or healthy or wise. They wondered at God's commands as sometimes I do. Even the disciple who loved Jesus most didn't always understand everything he did or taught. Realizing this allows me to have moments of depression; it allows me to cry and pound my fists on God's chest. It allows me to be the person I am because I am God's person. I can look to my Creator because I am his. I can look to my Redeemer; I can look ahead to fulfillment and to deliverance. And I can be happy even in my "failures," waiting to see how these too will be used because I am secure in the One who made me and owns me.

I know that there is a tomorrow. I understand with David that my mistakes do not end my usefulness for all time. I know with Peter that even denial is not permanent. I see and know and believe with the Apostle Paul that even "if we are faithless, he will remain faithful, for he cannot disown himself" (2 Timothy 2:13).[5]

There is a tomorrow. Experience it as a chosen person.

❦ P R A Y E R ❦

Dear Lord,

Thank You for the renewal You have begun in me. Help me discover the extent of this renewal and envision what You see me becoming.

Help me move from living my life stuck in yesterdays to the freedom of what You have for me today and tomorrow.

May I take the risk of becoming a risk-taker while grasping Your hand for strength and confidence. Give my fears and hesitations wings to fly away so I may discover my freedom and blessing in You.

In Jesus' name. Amen.

CHAPTER NINE

Yes, You Can Change!

As I work with people in counseling, a standard question almost always surfaces: "Norm, do you think I can really change?" Often what they're saying is, "Yes, I think I want to change. But I don't want to get my hopes up again and see them crushed. I want to change, but I'm afraid to try."

Why are people afraid of change? Why are they afraid to try?

First, there is a certain amount of stability in living your life unchanged even with your pain or problems. There is strange comfort in the familiar, even when it hurts. You disrupt this stability when you make a change. For example, why do some women marry men who are like their critical and abusive fathers? Because that's what they know best. They are comfortable.

But change is a part of life. It's inevitable. Isn't it better to hope for change, plan for change, and have a voice in what takes place? Your enemy is not change itself but not believing in the possibility of change.

Other people are afraid to change because they see change as an admission of failure. In order to change they have to admit to themselves and perhaps to other people,

"The way I've been living is wrong," and they hate admitting they're wrong.

But it is actually a sign of maturity to admit that you want your life to be different. Changing means that you want the present to be different from the past, that you are preparing for the future, that you are adapting to new situations, and that you desire growth. Your world is changing, and you want to keep up with it and even affect some of its changes. You want to become a tomorrow person rather than a yesterday person. That's a mature outlook on life of a person who acknowledges he or she is chosen for blessing.

Still other people resist change because they don't want to be controlled or scheduled. "Change should be natural and spontaneous," they say. "This feels like work. Change should just 'flow' from us and not be something we have to plan."

But whether or not we are aware of it, we make large and small choices for change all day long at work, at home, in our relationships, in our problem-solving. We are not as spontaneous and free as we would like to think we are. Most changes that are worth anything require planning, personal discipline, and just plain work.

Some people resist change because they are fearful that experimenting with change will produce a negative result. Granted, change is risky, and there are no guarantees as to the outcome. Some changes can make matters worse, but that's part of the risk. Actually, the likelihood that positive changes will take place when we attempt them is quite high. If change is to occur, you need to be flexible and willing to run a risk.

Everyone makes choices about changing. But sometimes the choices are in the wrong direction. Tim Hansel tells about a close friend of his who flew back for his 40-year high school reunion. His friend was excitedly anticipating seeing all the changes that had occurred in his classmates and hearing about all their accomplishments.

He wondered if any of them had been profoundly changed by Christ as he had been.

When Tim met his friend at the airport after the reunion, the man seemed almost despondent. Tim writes:

Finally I said, "Well, how was the reunion?"

"Tim," the man said, "it was one of the saddest experiences of my life."

"Good grief," I said, more than a little surprised. "What happened?"

"It wasn't what happened but what didn't happen. It has been forty years, forty years—and they haven't changed. They had simply gained weight, changed clothes, gotten jobs...but they hadn't really changed. And what I experienced was maybe one of the most tragic things I could ever imagine about life. For reasons I can't fully understand, it seems as though some people choose not to change."

There was a long silence as we walked back to the car. On the drive home, he turned to me and said, "I never, never want that to be said of me, Tim. Life is too precious, too sacred, too important. If you ever see me go stagnant like that, I hope you give me a quick, swift kick where I need it—for Christ's sake. I hope you'll love me enough to challenge me to keep growing."[1]

Listen to Yourself Talk

We've spent quite a bit of time learning to let go of the past and move toward the future. You understand now that believing you must remain handcuffed and crippled by certain situations and issues in life is a myth. It's an unbiblical viewpoint. But believing that change is possible and that you can move ahead in your life is a healthy, biblical viewpoint.

As you grow and change you may need to exchange certain negative attitudes and ways of talking to yourself for new attitudes and self-talk that will help you approach the challenge of change from a position of strength. Here are some examples of phrases that may try to creep in and spoil your commitment to growth:

- "I can't..."
- "That's a problem."
- "I'll never..."
- "That's awful!"
- "Why is life this way?"
- "If only..."
- "Life is a big struggle."
- "What will I do?"

These are victim phrases. We hear so much today about people being victimized by someone else. But there are more people who are victimized by their own beliefs and attitudes. By using phrases like these, you reinforce the control that problems or hurts have over your life. Every time you think or say one of these phrases, you subconsciously begin to believe it and fulfill it. You eventually talk yourself into believing that these phrases represent the truth, and thus you become a victim of your beliefs.

Let's consider what happens when you exchange victim phrases for words that better express your position of blessing in Christ.

"I can't." How many times a day do you say these words? Have you ever kept track? Do you realize that these words are prompted by some kind of unbelief, fear, or lack of hope? Think about it. These three factors often hinder us from moving on with our lives.

When you say "I can't," you are saying that you have no control over your life. It's no harder to say, "It's worth a try," and you'll like the results of this positive phrase much better.

"That's a problem." Sometimes instead of saying "That's a problem," we say "He's a problem" or "She's a

problem." People who see life's complications as problems or burdens are immersed in fear and hopelessness. Life is full of barriers and detours. But with every obstacle comes an opportunity to learn and grow—if you hold the right attitude. Using other phrases such as "That's a challenge" or "That's an opportunity for learning something new" leaves the door open for moving ahead.

"I'll never..." This victim phrase is the anchor of personal stagnation. It's the signal of unconditional surrender to what exists or has happened in your life. It doesn't give yourself or God an opportunity. Instead say "I've never considered that before" or "I haven't tried it, but I'm willing to try" and open the door to personal growth.

"That's awful." Sometimes this phrase is appropriate in view of the shocking, dire situations we often hear about in the news. But those events are extraordinary. In everyday experiences, "That's awful" is an inappropriate overreaction that holds us back. Make it a point to eliminate its usage for life's everyday problems. Instead, respond by saying "Let's see what we can do about this situation" or "I wonder how I can help at this time" or "I wonder how I can do this differently."

"Why is life this way?" This is a normal response to the deep pains and sudden shocks of life. Some people experience one hurt and disappointment after another. Others experience a major setback and choose to linger in its crippling aftermath without recovering. They inappropriately use this question over and over again for months and years.

"Why is life this way?" and its companion statement, "Life isn't fair," are overused for the normal, minor upsets of everyday life. Life is unpredictable. Life is unfair. Life isn't always the way we want it to be. But our response to life is our choice, and the healthiest response is reflected in James 1:2-3: "Consider it wholly joyful, my brethren, whenever you are enveloped in or encounter trials of any sort, or fall into various temptations. Be assured and understand that the trial and proving of your faith bring out endurance and steadfastness and patience" (AMP).

These verses encourage us to make up our minds to regard adversity as something to welcome or be glad about. Joy in life is a choice. Growth in life is a choice. Change in life can be a choice, and choice comes before joy, growth, and change.

"If only..." This phrase makes us yesterday people and imprisons us in lost dreams. I hear it constantly from couples in counseling who are stuck with unfulfilled dreams or expectations. They keep themselves bottled up with their "if only's."

But there is another phrase that can release us from yesterday and usher us into the future. The phrase "Next time" shows that we have given up our regrets, we have learned from past occurrences, and we are getting on with our lives.

"Life is a big struggle." This victim phrase reinforces the difficulties of life. Struggles can and should be turned into adventures. Yes, it will take work. You may be stretched, and you may feel uncomfortable for a time. But this is the way to take steps forward.

"What will I do?" This question is a cry of despair coupled with fear of the future and the unknown. Instead say, "I don't know what I can do at this moment, but I know I can handle this. Thank God I don't have to face this issue by myself. I can learn and become a different person." Remember the encouraging words in Philippians 4:13 and Jeremiah 29:11: "I can do everything through him who gives me strength"; "'For I know the plans I have for you,' declares the Lord, 'plans to prosper you and not to harm you, plans to give you hope and a future.'"

Are You Changeable?

What's your track record for seeing your dreams become reality? How are you doing when it comes to making choices and, ultimately, changes in your life? How many successes and failures have you had? Are you making progress? How much? Let's evaluate where you are.

In the space provided, list six choices you've made in the past 10 years, three which led to a successful change and three which did not. Any kind of changes can be listed.

Choices for Change

1.

2.

3.

4.

5.

6.

Now answer each of the following questions for each choice you listed:

1. What prompted you to make your choice?

2. Did you have several alternatives available to you at that time?

3. Did you list the consequences of your choice and consider your resources for making that choice a reality?

4. In what way was the will of God considered in this choice?

5. Did you make this choice freely, or were you pressured or coerced by others? If so, who influenced you?

6. Describe your feelings following your choice.

7. Did you stick to your original decision, or did you make alterations along the way?

8. In what way was this choice a vision?

9. How did your failures differ from your successes? How did you turn your failures into learning experiences? What will you do differently next time?

Jesus Christ, the Change Agent

Change is possible for you if you have a relationship with Jesus Christ. Why? Because faith in Christ is a life of continuing inward change that leads to outward change. Allowing Him to change us on the inside is the starting point. Paul wrote, "I am again in the pains of childbirth until *Christ is formed in you*" (Galatians 4:19, emphasis added). He was telling us that we must let Jesus Christ live in and through us. When you grasp the fact that Christ is working inside you, your hope will soar for the changes you desire to make.

In Ephesians 4:23-24 we are told, "Be made new in the attitude of your minds;... put on the new self, created to be like God in true righteousness and holiness." The new self must be put on from the inside. We are able to put on the new self because God has placed Jesus Christ within us. We are to let Him work within us. This means we must give Him access to those "impossible" concerns in our lives that need to be changed. What door do you need to open in your life today to allow Christ to work?

When you accepted Christ, you became a new creation in Jesus Christ. You are now identified with Him. In 2 Corinthians 5:17, Paul says, "Therefore, if anyone is in Christ, he is a new creation; the old has gone, the new has come!" Then in Romans 6:6 he says, "Our old self was crucified with him... that we should no longer be slaves to sin." By believing in Jesus Christ, we have died with Him and have been raised a new creation with Him. All things are new.

In what way are you new today?

In what way do you want to be new today?

In what way can you be new today?

How can your mind—your thought life—and the influence of past experiences become new in your life now? First Corinthians 2:16 tells us, "We have the mind of Christ," and in 1 Corinthians 1:30 we read, "Christ Jesus, who has become for us wisdom from God." We have the mind of Christ and God's wisdom to help us apply it to the choices and changes that need to take place in our lives. Now, that's hope!

❦ P R A Y E R ❦

Dear Lord,

I don't want to be handcuffed by confining victim phrases. Take from me any inclination to think or say, "I can't," "If only...," "I'll never," or "It's a problem." Help me realize how these beliefs put a damper on all You have for me.

Thank You, Father, for Your wisdom and for the help You will give me in using the mind of Jesus in my life. Help me make the choice to change where You show me I need to change. Thank You for being the God of hope. Thank You for choosing me for blessing.

In Jesus' name. Amen.

CHAPTER TEN

Moving Ahead with Hope and Faith

Frustration. No one said a word. They didn't have to. Their faces said it all. Four men with four different expressions of frustration. The fifth man, a friend of theirs, was lying near them patiently and passively. But what else could he do in his condition? He was paralyzed.

The four men heard that Jesus was in their town. They knew He was the one who could heal their friend. All they had to do was carry their friend to Him. But when they arrived at the home where Jesus was teaching, their hopes faded. People—crowds of people—pushed and shoved, taking up every inch of space. They couldn't get inside the house to the One who could touch their friend.

They were silent and frustrated as they stood in that narrow, dusty street. They were so near yet so far from Jesus. Did this mean they were defeated in their quest? Were they ready to give up on the blessing they sought? They wondered, struggled, and thought, looking at one another for an answer. They all wanted the paralytic to be healed. They wanted him to walk with them, fish with them, travel with them.

If we had been there at that very time in history and had asked the question, "How hopeful are you that you'll get your friend into the house to see Jesus today? How great

125

is your faith?" what would they have said? Perhaps they would have said nothing, preferring to answer us by what they did. Let's pick up the story as recreated by one of the finest inspirational writers of our time, Ken Gire:

> Not to be denied, the determined men back off and brainstorm another approach. "The stairs. What about the outside stairs to the roof?"
>
> Their enthusiasm mounts with every step they ascend. When they reach the top, their hearts are pounding in their throats. Laying their friend down, they survey the roof to pinpoint where Jesus is standing. Then, with adrenalin pumping, they remove the clay tiles and begin burrowing.
>
> The falling debris creates a billowy cloud of dust and sends the crowd scooting back, coughing their complaints into their hands.
>
> Their eyes angle upward, and the first thing they see is a tangle of fingers worming their way to widen the hole. They see a shaft of sunlight, a pair of eyes searching for Jesus, then four pairs of hands widening the hole, and finally, the bottom of the paralytic's mat.
>
> The friends strain to lower the paralyzed man as several men below stretch to ease the mat to the floor.
>
> From the opening in the roof spills an inverted funnel of light, where flecks of dust pirouette in an evanescent ballet, dancing spritely around the limp man on the floor.
>
> Jesus' eyes are transfixed on the four heads circling the hole in the ceiling. The text says he "saw their faith." Their faith. The faith of the paralytic's friends. It is on the wings of their faith that the mercy from heaven descends.[1] (See Mark 2:1-12.)

As this biblical narrative illustrates, hope-filled faith is the pathway to blessing. Hope and faith keep us growing and help us become risk-takers. Hope and faith encourage us to make the choice for change. Hope and faith help us realize the blessing for which we have been chosen.

If you were in my office seeking counsel concerning a change you would like to see happen in your life, how high would be your level of hope and faith that change will happen? Five percent? Twenty percent? Fifty percent? Ninety percent? The amount of hope and faith we have directly affects our capacity for change and blessing.

You've Got to Have Hope

I sat looking at the marital inventory that had been completed and mailed back to me by a couple coming in the next day for marital counseling. I was concerned because one of the two had answered the question, "How hopeful are you about resolving the issues in your marriage?" with the response, "Very little hope." I can understand the discouragement that some people feel, but when there is little or no hope it is difficult to change.

We use the word hope so glibly. It's also easy to misuse it. Have you ever said, "I hope it comes in the mail today" or "I hope I get that raise" or "I hope they are able to visit us this year"? Every time we use the word hope in that way we are expressing a desire, but we are also wishing for something that is uncertain. In a way we are saying, "I don't know for certain if this is going to happen. It might or might not, but I wish it would."

That's not the biblical definition of hope. In the Scriptures, hope is solid, sure. It is a certainty. There are no maybe's or I hope so's about it. In the Bible, "hope is man's eager expectation of something that God has promised will certainly happen in the future."[2]

There's no question that God's promises will be kept. They are certain.

127

Hope is not blind optimism; it's realistic optimism. A person of hope is always aware of the struggles and difficulties of life, but he lives beyond them with a sense of potential and possibility. He is not an impossibility thinker.

A person of hope doesn't just live for the possibilities of tomorrow but sees the possibilities of today, even when it's not going well.

A person of hope doesn't just long for what he's missing in his life but experiences what he has already received.

A person of hope can say an emphatic *no* to stagnation and an energetic *yes* to life. Hope is allowing God's Spirit to set us free and draw us forward in our lives.

Listen to the story one man told me after he chose to become a man of hope:

> For years I limped through life. Other people saw me as happy, successful, and satisfied. What a joke! My life was pain—just pain inside. And I was very clever at hiding it from my friends. I moved through life smiling on the outside and agonizing on the inside. I felt hopeless that my inner life would ever change. For years it did not change.
>
> But now I can tell you that a person doesn't have to go through life with crippling hurts and frustrations controlling his life. I made the choice to change, and my life did begin to change, gradually at first. But now I am free to live as God wants me to live.

This man laid hold of the hope we have in Christ and found a way to free himself from the problems and pain of his life. You may be feeling as he did at first, that you're stuck and that hope is an illusion. Wrong! Hope is a reality. It is available to help you choose and change and be blessed.

Choose Hope

I've heard people say that having hope is a matter of one's personality type. Some are born more hopeful than others. But is that really true? No. Hope is a choice. It is an option. Many things happen in life over which we have no control, but we do have control over how we respond to them. When we have hope, some of the pain of a circumstance is eased because we are looking beyond the situation to what will happen in the future. And even if the situation cannot be changed, our response to it can change. We can choose to take charge of the situation rather than be victimized by it.

Hope is not something we generate by ourselves. It happens because our focus is on who God is and how He perceives us. Hope comes as we move ahead. When we take our eyes off of Christ, our hope can erode. When hope erodes it causes us to give up, fold, cave in, or live with resignation. Sometimes the erosion of hope is like an avalanche that is over in 20 seconds. A negative experience hits us hard, and our hope suddenly goes flat. At other times hope erodes so gradually that we're not even aware of it. We just go through life with no ambition, feeling unblessed.

I see hopeless-feeling people in my office every week. There are so many times when I wish I could reach out and give these people hope. We can become so despondent and discouraged that we must rely upon the hope of others to carry us along until our own hope returns or develops. If you have ever been depressed you know what it feels like to have no hope. Hopelessness is at the core of depression.

But hope can grow. Often it means not letting your situation or circumstances control you. When we are discouraged and hurt, God is still alive and still loves us, even if we don't feel His love.

Hope can reign in the midst of calamity if we have nurtured it in our lives. I've always enjoyed the book by Robert Veninga, *A Gift of Hope*. In it he recounts the story of a woman who had every right to give up but refused to do so. Here is her story:

Marie Fisher was brought to a hospice to die. Seven thousand rays of high energy radiation could not stop the cancer from spreading throughout her body. The hospice seemed to be the last stop for this frail fifty-three-year-old woman, depleted after months of therapy.

Upon being escorted to her room Marie made the observation that, while everyone expected her to die, it wasn't exactly what she had in mind. With a hint of fire in her eyes she informed the head nurse that she was going to get well. What's more, she intended to leave the hospice not in a wheelchair, but on her own strength.

Two days later Marie's health was rapidly failing. A nurse speculated that her heart was simply giving out. She developed a severe breathing disorder and there was general recognition that she wouldn't last out the night.

Marie, however, would not cooperate with death. Deep in her being was a tenacious hold on life that was more powerful than the forces that were pushing her to die.

An oncologist who was monitoring her condition shook his head in disbelief as he listened to a heartbeat that grew steadily stronger. A nurse noted that the vital signs were beginning to stabilize. When it was announced that Marie's blood pressure had reached $110/80$, a quiet cheer went up in her room. "She simply wouldn't give up," said her physician.

In the weeks that followed, Marie was determined to get out of bed and walk a few steps every day. She was equally determined to set new goals for herself, for, after all, there were people she wanted to see and a huge stack of paperback novels that needed to be read.

But then came the setback. The cancer had spread into her pancreas. Not even high doses of morphine could control the pain.

An oncologist indicated that a surgical procedure might alleviate some of the discomfort. "However," he cautioned, "you should know that you are not a good surgical risk. Just getting you through the anesthetic would be an accomplishment."

Alone with her thoughts, Marie examined her options. An hour later she signed the forms permitting the surgery to take place. She reasoned there was a pretty good chance that the surgery might bring relief. More important, it might give her added life. The next day she successfully completed a three-hour operation.

While there was no sign of remission, Marie's bodily functions gradually returned to normal. "I'm feeling stronger every week," she confided to a roommate. Soon she was walking with little pain. Then she abandoned her hospital gown in favor of street clothes, for, as she told a nurse, "A hospital gown is a symbol of sickness." And then she asked the question that had been on her mind ever since she had entered the hospice: "When can I go home?"

"I'll never forget the day Marie left the hospice," said Catherine Holmberg, the chief nurse in the unit. "Marie was radiant. She put on a bright red dress accented with a white scarf. You could tell that she was proud of every step she was taking. If there was any pain she wasn't going to tell anybody about it. "The word quickly spread that Marie was leaving. The patients came out of their rooms and the nurses stopped all their tasks as they watched her walk down the hall with her head held high. Then someone started to clap. Pretty soon we all joined in. A few tears ran down the cheeks of some of the nurses. All we could do was marvel at her courage. She had survived."[3]

Depending on God for Hope

This woman made a choice to have hope. But how can a person who has little hope develop more hope? It's simpler than you might think. Become dependent on God and give up some of your independence. Radical? Perhaps. Contrary to what is being propagated in society today? Perhaps. Hope means going to God with every decision, every venture, and every challenge. For example, I've learned over the past years to ask God, "What would You have me write? Is this a book I should be writing or not?" I want Him involved in this area of my life as well as every other area. And so I must depend on Him to guide and direct me in the large and small dimensions of my life.

I like what Barry Johnson says about depending on God for hope:

> Only when I release control does God take control; only when I consent to follow the Spirit do I find the Spirit.

> And so it is with choosing hope. Tomorrow is a river, filled with unexpected developments, constantly on the move, never to be trapped, never to be mastered. In that knowledge, ours is the challenge to admit our incompetency and claim the guidance of the Holy Spirit. For believers, until we confess what we cannot achieve, we will never know what we can. Until we choose tomorrow, we cannot release tomorrow. And until we release tomorrow, we cannot fully experience today.[4]

Your hope and mine must be centered on God and His working in our lives. When we hit difficult times in life, our dependent grasp on God will make the difference. Johnson says:

> The core of our hope is God's unfailing concern for us. Even when it appears we have been forsaken, we must

trust the future to the one who knows us by name and rise above our despair. What is our purpose? Paul said it: "For me, to live is Christ and to die is gain." Our purpose is to center in the risen Lord and look at every aspect of life from that lofty perch. Our purpose is to choose hope.

Christ knows about the trauma with our jobs, the pain in our marriages, the gaps between us and our children, and our frazzled nerves. Like the hairs of our heads, so our troubles are numbered. Knowing this, we must release them to his care and get on with our living.

What we're talking about here is a matter of perspective. God has never promised to meet all our expectations. It is foolhardy to assume that a relationship with the Lord will deliver a person from all trauma. Problems still develop. Tragedy continues to strike. Confusion rears its ugly head. Nevertheless, that person who chooses hope remains one notch above all this nonsense. The purpose smothers the pain.[5]

Faith Is the Victory

Faith is the inseparable twin of hope in helping us choose change and growth and find blessing. As the story of the paralytic in Mark 2 illustrates, when you have hope and faith, you don't just sit back and allow life to happen. You're involved in the process. The four men took their crippled friend to Jesus. When they couldn't get through the crowd, they didn't give up. Their hope and faith prompted them to tear up the roof to lay hold of the blessing they knew was theirs.

Faith changes lives, and in some cases it changes the world. Consider this:

• We used to believe it was impossible to break the sound barrier in flight. Test pilot Chuck Yeager shattered that belief.

• We used to believe it was a physical impossibility to run a four-minute mile. Roger Bannister shattered that belief.

• We used to believe it was impossible to fly nonstop across the Atlantic Ocean. Charles Lindbergh shattered that belief.

• We used to believe it was impossible to fly to the moon. Neil Armstrong shattered that belief when he took those first steps on the moon.

There are so many more myths and false beliefs that have been shattered. How did it happen? Because someone had the faith that things could be different.

One of the characteristics necessary for the unfolding of faith in our lives is perseverance. The faith of the paralytic's four friends reflected perseverance. This word is literally made up of two words, one meaning "to remain" and the other meaning "under." Perseverance is the ability to stick to something, to stay there regardless of what is happening. When pressures hit, some tend to give in and crumble rather than stand firm and conquer the pressure. The author of the book of Hebrews wrote to a group of people under pressure, "Therefore, since we are surrounded by such a great cloud of witnesses, let us throw off everything that hinders and the sin that so easily entangles, and let us run with perseverance the race marked out for us" (Hebrews 12:1).

An example of such perseverance is found in a group of people who take over the city of Los Angeles for a day in March each year. It happens on a Sunday morning, and we have learned to change our route to church on that day. This group is given the right of way on 26 miles of city streets. They come in all sizes, shapes, and ages. They are marathon runners and walkers.

Some entrants run the entire 26 miles, others run part of the race, then slow to a walk. Other participants walk most of the way, and still others push themselves in their wheelchairs. The earliest finishers arrive at their goal in less than three hours. There are others who arrive eight hours later, exhausted, feet blistered, sides aching, and partially dehydrated. But they finish. They don't fold. They don't give in to the pain. It doesn't matter to them that they finish in 4,587th place. All they want to achieve is to persevere and finish.

We too can persevere in the race of life because of the presence of Jesus Christ in our lives.

See Yourself Filled with Hope and Faith

Sometimes when I am working with a person who has no hope or faith, only an attitude of despair and failure, I ask him a series of unconventional questions to change his perspective. For example, one day I asked Jim, "How would you describe the way you view life right now. Is it positive or negative? Hopeful or despairing?"

His response was, "It's negative. I don't feel any hope at all."

"How long have you felt this way, Jim?"

"Probably about three years," Jim answered.

"So during that time you've had the opportunity to discover and experience what it's like to live with no hope and basically a negative outlook as you've described it to me."

"Well, yes."

Then I asked, "Jim, do you need any more time to discover or experience what it's like to live that way, especially after three years?"

Jim replied, "You make it sound like I have a choice in this."

"Well, what if you did have a choice? Have you ever considered that you might?"

"No, I guess I haven't, Norm."

"If you've already tested out one way to live and discovered the results, Jim, why not test out the opposite way and discover what that has to offer you? Do you really have anything to lose?"

"Well, not really. That's actually why I'm here, Norm. I don't like what's going on in my life. I want to change."

"Jim, you've just started the process by wanting to change. If you have hope that you can change, we can do something. It will take work, dependence on God and His Word, and a new way of measuring progress. But your desire to change is the beginning."

It sounds so simple, doesn't it? I realize that it isn't as simple as it sounds, but we can gain needed encouragement to begin living differently just by considering what could happen if we did live differently. After all, if you've tried something long enough to know the results, and you're not all that happy with the results, you know there must be a better way. And sometimes it takes a few radical questions or thoughts to prompt us to consider a new option.

I'll never forget something that was taught to me years ago by psychiatrist Dr. Leonard Zunnin. He told my classmates and me what he often shares with those who are depressed and without hope. He asks them what they do in the morning after they get up. Often he will hear someone answer, "Well, I don't get up very early. I usually get up about nine and shuffle off to the kitchen. I warm up some left-over coffee, and then turn on the news on TV. I usually keep the shades drawn, and I bum around in my pajamas until afternoon. Then, if I can find any decent food, I might fix a sandwich."

Dr. Zunnin replies with, "Friend, if I lived like that I'd be depressed too. In fact, I'd be even more depressed than you are. How do you do it? How do you keep yourself from being even more depressed than you are?"

With that odd last question he very subtly changes the direction of the person's thought life to consider how well he is functioning despite his depression. And for many this turn-about in their thinking begins to sink in and alter the direction of their depression.

We do have a choice of what we think about and focus upon. I hear this all the time as clients come in and complain about their problems and difficulties with a situation or their spouse. But when I ask, "What went well for you this week?" or "What did your partner do that you appreciated?" invariably they are able to come up with something. One astute client said, "I suppose you would prefer that I come in and share what went well this week rather than start with all the problems." My smile was all the answer he needed. And in several weeks his attitude began to become more hopeful. The basis for hope was there. He was just overlooking it.

We limit ourselves by our beliefs and thoughts. For many, the greatest prison of their life is the locked door of their mind. We become and act out the rehearsed script of our mind.

A number of years ago in a small town in the British Isles, a new jail was constructed that claimed to have an escape-proof cell. Harry Houdini, the great escape artist known all over the world, was invited to come and test it to see if it really was escape proof. He accepted the invitation, having once boasted that no jail could hold him.

Houdini entered the cell, and the jailor closed the door behind him. Houdini listened to the sound of the key being slipped into the lock. The jailor withdrew the key and left. Houdini took out his tools and started the process of working on that cell door. But it didn't work out the way he expected. Nothing seemed to work, and the hours passed. He was puzzled because he had never failed to open a locked door.

Finally the great Houdini admitted defeat. But when he leaned against the door in resigned exhaustion, it suddenly opened. The jailer had never locked it. The only place the door was locked was—you can guess—in Houdini's mind.

I've done it and so have you; we've locked ourselves in because of what we have thought and believed. As a result we lock ourselves away from the hope and faith that lead to blessing. Instead of enjoying the assurance and freedom that comes from belonging to God, we become the negative people we imagine ourselves to be. Nathaniel Hawthorne captured the dilemma beautifully in *The House of Seven Gables*: "What other dungeon is so dark as one's own heart! What jailer so inexorable as one's self!"

The only way to escape this dark dungeon and live in blessing is to begin living as a person of hope and faith. In letting go of the past and taking risks in the present, you will begin to see the faithfulness of the Lord at work in your own life. These experiences will become a reservoir of strength for you in the future.

❦ P R A Y E R ❦

Dear Lord,

Sometimes I feel just as disabled emotionally and spiritually as the paralytic was physically. My discouragement and depression sometimes feel so permanent that thoughts of being different are elusive.

Faith? I need more. Hope? I need more.

Help me choose both. Help me admit that I am incompetent in myself, and remind me to claim the guidance of Your Holy Spirit. I realize that You know the cause and source of discouragement. I commit these causes to You and ask You to take away their power to imprison me.

I want the perseverance that comes from a relationship with You. I thank You in advance for perseverance becoming a reality for me. I want to finish the race You've called me to run. Assist me in keeping the difficulties in my life in proper perspective and not turning them into giants.

In Jesus' name. Amen.

CHAPTER ELEVEN

Are You A Blessed Survivor?

U nderstanding that you are known and loved by God doesn't exempt you from difficulties and pain on earth. I work with many individuals who are experiencing major crises in their lives or are going through valleys of grief even though they have let go of the past and are moving toward the future. Some of them struggle on and on over an extended period of time. But others are able to pull through and turn their painful experiences into times of learning and growth. I call these people survivors. They are blessed.

If you're only looking for material and relational blessings, you may miss other significant ways in which God is blessing you. In fact you may not consider the trials and problems you encounter as blessings at all! But as long as what happens results in the true definition of a blessing—*the assurance that you belong to God*—it is indeed a blessing for you.

Often other people, and our experiences with these people, can be instruments God uses as a source of blessing. For example, our retarded son Matthew was a tremendous source of blessing to my wife and me. Our values, perspective on life, character qualities, insights, skills, and relationship with God grew and were refined because of the presence of this handicapped child in our lives.

On March 15, 1990, Matthew was called home, and we have an empty place in our lives. He was 23 years old physically, but only about 18 months old mentally. Because of the severity of his retardation, Matthew spoke only a few words and made very few responses. We only have one brief film of him and no audio tape recordings. Beside these, all we have left of Matthew are memories, and anything that adds to this storehouse is valued so much.

God's blessings through Matthew's life have continued even since his death. For example, as this chapter was being written, August 15 came. It was the day we would have observed Matthew's twenty-fourth birthday, and our sense of loss was fresh.

That evening we made contact with an attendant who cared for Matthew at Salem Christian Home where he lived for the last 11 years of his life. A friend told us that this woman had some experiences with Matthew she wanted to share with us.

As we talked with her over the phone, she told us about several features of Matthew's life we hadn't heard about. She said he learned to put a very simple puzzle together. This was news to us. She told us that when she took him for a walk outside, he would walk way ahead of her and try to hide from her. We hadn't seen that side of Matthew. She shared how he had learned to hold the hair dryer to dry his hair and how he would turn it around and blow it on her hair.

One of the most incredible stories the attendant recounted (at least it was incredible to us) was Matthew's response when she brought her six-month-old baby into the school dorm. Despite the limitations of the retarded children, the attendant let each of them hold her child. To our surprise, she said that when Matthew held this little baby in his arms and rocked him while she sang "Rock-a-bye Baby," tears trickled down Matthew's face.

To someone who has never had the experience of raising a handicapped child, this might not seem like much. But with Matthew's limitations so massive and the "ordinary" experiences of his daily life so rare, knowing about these things our son did is a blessing for us.

Qualities for Survival

The people I call "blessed survivors" have a number of characteristics in common. Those who handle life's difficulties most effectively and are best equipped to move ahead in life work at developing the following traits. We touched on a few of them in the chapters on putting the past behind, but they also apply to dealing with difficult situations on a day-to-day basis.

1. Survivors tend to plan ahead in order to effectively handle the transitions of life. Losses and crises come into every life as unwelcome guests. Survivors anticipate the possibility of future problems and make plans to handle what may happen. They make plans for coping, and they stick with their plans.

Have you anticipated some of the difficulties you will face in the next few years? It could be anything from an unexpected move, a business failure, a death in the family, a child leaving home early, or an adult child returning home. Do you have a plan for handling these "surprises"?

2. When it is not possible to plan ahead, survivors learn from others who have gone through difficult times in life. Who do you know who has survived difficulties and grown through the experience? It may be someone you know personally or someone you read about like Joni Erickson-Tada, who is paralyzed, or Dave Dravecky, the major league baseball player whose arm and shoulder were amputated in 1991 because of cancer.

3. Survivors have found healthy ways to express hurt, anger, and resentment. They don't bottle up their hurt feelings, nor do they complain and force their discomfort on others. How do you deal with your feelings? Are you a complainer?

4. Survivors do not live independently. They have learned to draw on their own strengths and gifts and use them effectively, yet they still ask for and can accept assistance from others. They can also express concern and warmth to others. Whom do you rely on? Have you ever inventoried your own personal strengths and gifts to better understand why you need others?

5. Survivors have role models they can look to. They gain inner strength from knowing about these people and what they have done. Who are your role models? Have you ever done a study of the great men of Scripture to learn from their example? What can you learn from Joseph, Abraham, Isaac, David, Elijah, Jeremiah, and the others?

6. Survivors are people who desire to learn and grow. They hope to continue growing throughout their lives. How are you growing at this present time in your life? What are you consciously doing so your learning will continue?

7. Survivors accept responsibility for making things happen in their lives. They face and attempt to overcome obstacles. They avoid blame. What about you? What have you overcome? What are you overcoming? Does blame dominate your thinking, or is it just a fleeting visitor from time to time?

8. Survivors are optimistic, and during tough times their optimism prevails. Are you optimistic or pessimistic? Which way do you lean, especially during difficult times?

9. Survivors enjoy life. They can still laugh during the rough spots. Is the gift of laughter a characteristic of you as well?

10. Survivors have learned to use the trials and crises of life to grow stronger and wiser. Can you think of an example of this quality in your own life?

11. Survivors are flexible, resilient, and adaptable. These characteristics help us work through life experiences. The more rigid a person is, the less hopeful his life is, because rigidity makes changing direction difficult. Which of these words would others use to characterize you: rigid or flexible? Perhaps you should ask your spouse or a trusted friend if you're unsure.

12. Survivors don't give up. Courage and determination are their bywords. I hope they are your bywords also, because they reflect a person of hope and faith.[1]

Attitudes for Survival

Sometimes we think of survivors as being extraordinary individuals. A few are, but most are not. People of hope and faith have their faults and flaws. They are like anyone else—with one exception. They have some different ways of thinking. Here is a reminder of some of the attitudes that characterize blessed survivors.

1. "I will examine the future and let it guide what I do in the present." Many people, upon reaching middle age or old age, move into despair. They have regrets over the way they have lived and realize there is little time left to change anything. Perhaps by examining our priorities and values at a younger age we can gain better direction for our lives and be satisfied in later years.

According to the Scriptures, living life with a forward view is healthy and hopeful. Jesus said: "Most assuredly, I say to you, he who believes in Me, the works that I do he will do also; and greater works than these he will do, because I go to my Father. And whatever you ask in My name, that I will do, that the Father may be glorified in the Son. If you ask anything in My name, I will do it" (John 14:12-14, NKJV).

145

God asked Abraham to look into the future. In Genesis 13:14-16 He instructed Abraham to gaze northward, southward, eastward, and westward at the land He was giving to him. Then in verse 17 God told Abraham, then called Abram, to do something very strange: "Arise, walk about the land through its length and breadth; for I will give it to you" (NASB). Dr. Lloyd Ogilvie comments:

> In order to build in Abram the confidence of a risk-taker, the Lord had to help him claim the reality of the seemingly impossible. He not only gave him a vision, but he also made him walk through that vision until he made it really his own.
>
> God does the same thing with you and me. First he gives us the impossible dream, then he helps us envision what it will be like to possess our possession, and then through our imagination he helps us persistently image the reality. What is the dream for you?[2]

Have you examined your future? Will you today?

2. *"No matter what happens, I will not allow myself to be defeated.* I will keep on trying and will not give up." Perseverance is a mark of hope and faith. It is essential to realizing blessing. Do you persevere and keep on trying?

3. *"I am a fortunate person regardless of what I have experienced."* There are blessings around you that you may be ignoring because you are focusing on your losses instead of your gains. There is always hope and the possibility of growth. You could be much worse off than you are. Survivors consistently take inventory of what they have rather than what they do not have. When was the last time you took such an inventory?

4. *"I will take advantage of every available opportunity."* I have talked to handicapped people who look for every opportunity to create and grow. Perhaps the more handicapped someone is, the more he appreciates what he can experience. We need to look at life through thankful eyes and seize the opportunities before us. What opportunities are around you right now that you could take

advantage of and use to generate even more hope for yourself?

5. *"I can accept my imperfections and learn to enjoy life and give to others."* Survivors don't strive for perfectionism. They realize it's impossible to be perfect. But they do work toward excellence. What are your imperfections? Do you dwell on these deficits, or do you direct your energy into improving what can be improved while accepting what can't be changed?

6. *"I can find meaning in situations and events that involve suffering or great loss."* Where meaninglessness exists, there is no hope, no sense of blessing. Sometimes the meaning of a negative or hurtful event cannot be seen at first but is discovered in time. Over a period of 23 years my wife and I learned this lesson and this attitude through the life and death of our retarded son, Matthew.

We must grieve our losses, but then we must come to the point of replacing our "why" questions with "how" questions: "How can I learn through this experience? How can I grow through this? How can others be helped through this? How can God be glorified through this experience?" What experience of suffering or loss are you facing at this time for which you need to find meaning? How do you think this can happen?

7. *"I will not allow myself to behave as a victim."* Even in the midst the hurt and pain of life, survivors learn to move on and choose not to see themselves as helpless victims. This involves a change in thinking for most people. Do you see yourself as a victim? If so, does this attitude create more victim experiences for you?

8. *"I am determined to keep pushing ahead."* Survivors are able to make and keep commitments. They are able to build their lives on Jeremiah 29:11 and 33:3 and allow God to guide them: "For I know the thoughts that I think toward you, says the Lord, thoughts of peace and not of evil, to give you a future and a hope" (NKJV); "Call to Me,

and I will answer you, and show you great and mighty things, which you do not know" (NKJV). In what ways are you living in the past? In what ways are you determinedly moving ahead in life?

9. *"I am willing to grow and change and learn new roles."* I often see this attitude in divorced persons as they learn to function as both Mom and Dad to their children. I see this in men who are able to learn to be affectionate, feeling-oriented, and demonstrative in relationships. Every one of us has an opportunity to grow and expand. If we don't, our only option is stagnation. In what ways are you growing and changing? In what ways do you need to expand in order to help yourself and those around you?

10. *"I want to be involved with people who will build me up and help me grow."* We were never meant to make it alone. But we are foolish to surround ourselves with people who fill us with negative talk and example. You can't grow and be blessed if you spend all your time with sick people. Healthy people don't tear you down or drain you. You need people in your life to give you strength. You need encouragers in your life. Who are the significant people in your life, and in what ways do they help you mature and grow stronger? Who do you pray for? Who prays for you?

11. *"I can face the challenges of life and handle the stresses and crises of life without denying their existence or giving up."* I especially like the last attitude. It's not just what happens to us but how we respond to what happens to us that is so important. It's the ability to take James 1:2-3 and apply it to our lives: "Consider it pure joy, my brothers, whenever you face trials of many kinds, because you know that the testing of your faith develops perseverance." In what ways is this passage becoming part of your life?[3]

Lord of the Impossible

Thinking about these attitudes of survival brings to my mind the title of a book my pastor, Lloyd Ogilvie, wrote a number of years ago: *Lord of the Impossible*. If that title doesn't speak to you about survival, hope, and blessing, I'm not sure what would.

There are many people who choose to live by hope who don't have a relationship with God through His Son, Jesus Christ. But how much more possible it is to be hopeful when we have a relationship with Him. And hope is the prelude for experiencing fully the blessings of God.

Perhaps you are still feeling and thinking that your situation, background, or circumstances are impossible. Humanly speaking, they may be. And yet we serve the God of the impossible. There's a lot I can't do by myself, but all things become possible when I'm in the presence of and follow the guidance of God. Survival is possible. Hope is available. He is Lord of the impossible.

Perhaps the starting point for developing your hope is in allowing the truth about hope from God's Word to saturate and penetrate your life. Would you allow that to occur in your life as I am allowing it to occur in mine? Would you journey with me into God's Word?

I would like you to do something for two weeks. Two weeks is just 14 days, and yet this brief assignment can radically change your attitude and outlook. It's very simple. Read each of the following passages aloud every day for the next two weeks. Read them with feeling. Read them with emphasis. Grasp their meaning and significance. Then reflect on your outlook. Experience the blessings that will come from these words.

> We have peace with God through our Lord Jesus Christ, through whom we have gained access by faith into this grace in which we now stand. And we rejoice in the hope of the glory of God (Romans 5:1-2).
>
> For in this hope we were saved. But hope that is seen is no hope at all. Who hopes for what he already has? But

149

if we hope for what we do not yet have, we wait for it patiently (Romans 8:24-25).

May the God of hope fill you with all joy and peace as you trust in him, so that you may overflow with hope by the power of the Holy Spirit (Romans 15:13).

And now these three remain: faith, hope and love. But the greatest of these is love (1 Corinthians 13:13).

By faith we eagerly await through the Spirit the righteousness for which we hope (Galatians 5:5).

I pray also that the eyes of your heart may be enlightened in order that you may know the hope to which he has called you, the riches of his glorious inheritance in the saints (Ephesians 1:18).

We have heard of your faith in Christ Jesus and of the love you have for all the saints—the faith and love that spring from the hope that is stored up for you in heaven and that you have already heard about in the word of truth, the gospel (Colossians 1:4-5).

God has chosen to make known among the Gentiles the glorious riches of this mystery, which is Christ in you, the hope of glory (Colossians 1:27).

Paul, an apostle of Christ Jesus by the command of God our Savior and of Christ Jesus our hope (1 Timothy 1:1).

The grace of God ... teaches us to say "No" to ungodliness and worldly passions, and to live self-controlled, upright and godly lives in this present age while we wait for the blessed hope—the glorious appearing of our great God and Savior, Jesus Christ (Titus 2:11-13).

We have this hope as an anchor for the soul, firm and secure. It enters the inner sanctuary behind the curtain, where Jesus, who went before us, has entered on our behalf (Hebrews 6:19-20).

Therefore, prepare your minds for action; be self-controlled; set your hope fully on the grace to be given you when Jesus Christ is revealed (1 Peter 1:13).

Two weeks. Pray that God will write these truths upon your heart, and then see what happens!

Dear Lord,

I want to be a survivor in all situations. I want to continue to learn and grow.

Help me be more diligent in planning for the future.

Give me positive and courageous people to learn from.

Keep me from stifling my emotions. Help me share them in a healthy ways.

May I not be a blamer, but may I take responsibility for my choices and actions.

Show me even more how to use the gift of laughter You've given to us all.

May I see problems and trials as growth-producing experiences.

May I live my life seeing You as the Lord of the impossible.

Thank You for giving me an attitude of hope and faith.

Thank you for choosing me for blessing.

In Jesus' name. Amen.

Part Four:

BLESSED TO BE A BLESSING

CHAPTER TWELVE

People—
God's Channels
of Blessing

A s a counselor, I am called to be a care-giver in the lives of those who come to me for help. It's a role I accept from the Lord as a ministry to others. But occasionally the roles in a counseling situation are dramatically reversed, as they were in my office recently.

Rick came in to talk to me about some problems he was having. In the course of our conversation, Rick noticed the latest photograph of my family displayed in my office. He asked about my family, and I mentioned that Matthew was now with the Lord. Rick asked a number of questions about Matthew and discovered how limited his abilities were. Then he said, "I guess you never experienced what most fathers experience with their sons, did you, Norm? You never played ball with Matthew, never took him fishing, and never heard him tell you what most sons say to their dads growing up. And you only experienced a few hugs from him, right?"

I nodded silently as tears began to fill my eyes at the fresh thoughts of Matthew.

Rick continued, "Well, just remember, Norm. When you die and arrive in heaven, your son Matthew will come running up to you and, with his newfound abilities, throw his arms around your neck and say, 'Daddy, I love you.'"

By then my tears were flowing freely. I said, "Thank you for saying that, Rick. No one has ever shared that with me before."

Rick smiled, got up, came over to me, and gave me a big hug. A new bond was established between us that day as I realized that counselees can also minister to counselors. I was deeply blessed by Rick's words and actions.

My experience with Rick illustrates the scriptural truth that other people are a primary channel through which God pours His blessing into our lives. It was Rick who tenderly encouraged me about seeing Matthew whole some day. And it was Rick who comforted me with a brotherly embrace. But as he did these things, he was really being Jesus to me. Later, as I listened to his problems and offered some helpful suggestions, I had the opportunity to be Jesus to Rick. And by allowing Jesus to minister in our midst, we both went away from the meeting blessed.

A Family of Blessing

Our relationship with others in the body of Christ is the source of some of the greatest blessings we receive. Remember: The essence of blessing is the assurance that we belong to God. Who can convey that assurance on earth better than someone in whom God lives? God is in heaven, but His body, those of us who have trusted in Christ and who are indwelt by His Spirit, is here on earth. When Jesus said, "Where two or three come together in my name, there am I with them" (Matthew 18:20), He wasn't talking about some mystical, out-of-body presence being with us. When two or three believers come together, because they belong to Christ and are indwelt by His Spirit, they become Jesus to one another. When Christians are together, the possibilities for God's blessing to flow are endless.

If you are a Christian, you are a member of the largest family on earth. It's the family of blessing, and it numbers into the millions. Some of your brothers and sisters are a different color than you. And if some of them spoke to you, you would not understand them, because they are from different cultures and speak different languages. But you are linked together with them because of the common bond of Jesus Christ.

Within the worldwide family of blessing are smaller, local families of believers called churches. Each group of Christians who worship and fellowship together regularly are called to be channels of God's blessing to each other. How? One way is by living out the "one anothers" of the New Testament. The one anothers of Scripture describe the lifestyle of mutual blessing within God's family. The Greek word for one another is used about 100 times in the New Testament. Does that give you some idea of how important it is for believers to bless one another?

Consider some of the ways we are to be blessing one another:

1. Mutual devotion: "Be devoted to one another in brotherly love" (Romans 12:10).

2. Preferential respect: "Honor one another above yourselves" (Romans 12:10).

3. Affirmation and encouragement: "Therefore encourage one another and build each other up, just as in fact you are doing" (1 Thessalonians 5:11).

4. Unity: "May the God who gives endurance and encouragement give you a spirit of unity among yourselves as you follow Christ Jesus" (Romans 15:5).

5. Acceptance: "Accept one another, then, just as Christ accepted you, in order to bring praise to God" (Romans 15:7).

6. Instruction: "I myself am convinced, my brothers, that you yourselves are full of goodness, complete in knowledge and competent to instruct one another" (Romans 15:14).

7. Mutual service: "Serve one another in love" (Galatians 5:13).

8. Mutual support: "Carry each other's burdens, and in this way you will fulfill the law of Christ" (Galatians 6:2).

9. Forgiveness and kindness: "Be kind and compassionate to one another, forgiving each other, just as in Christ God forgave you" (Ephesians 4:32).

10. Mutual submission: "Submit to one another out of reverence for Christ" (Ephesians 5:21).

When a brother or sister in Christ responds to you with devotion, honor, encouragement, acceptance, or kindness, what does it do for you? Doesn't it transmit a sense of God's love and the assurance that you belong to Him? That's how spiritual blessing is transmitted through ordinary flesh and blood. I need it. You need it. Others need it. When God said it wasn't good for us to be alone (see Genesis 2:18), perhaps He was thinking of the importance of people fellowshiping and worshiping together as a family of blessing.

Are you a source of blessing in your fellowship of believers? Are you receiving God's blessing through the ministry of others at your church? Reach out to your fellow believers. Open your life to them. God's blessings are there just waiting for you.

Friends—What a Blessing!

In a general sense, we are called to be care-givers to all who need us, especially the Christians around us. Paul wrote, "Therefore, as we have opportunity, let us do good to all people, especially to those who belong to the family of believers" (Galatians 6:10). But in addition to the larger family of blessing, God gives us special relationships with close, intimate friends whom we are to bless and who are to be a blessing to us. Jesus blessed the multitudes, but He maintained a closer relationship of friendship with His 12 disciples and an even tighter bond with Peter, James, and John. We need to nurture a core of close friendships through which we can give and receive blessing.

Friendships are more selective and reciprocal in commitment than our relationships with the members of our church in general. There is a vow of trust that exists in a friendship. There is no selfish competitiveness. Friends support one another and can count on one another.

Friendship involves mutual confidence, effort, and loyalty in the midst of differences. A friend is someone who hears your cry of pain and responds. A friend is someone who senses your struggle and is there to help carry the load. Proverbs 18:24 states, "There is a friend who sticks closer than a brother." If anyone should be a source of assurance that we belong to God and that He loves us and cares for us it should be our closest Christian friends.

If you are married, your primary source of the blessing of friendship is probably your spouse. As individuals we are incomplete in many ways. The friendship in our marriage relationship helps complete us. Everything God created in Genesis 1-2 was good and complete—except Adam without Eve (2:18). We all need helpers in life, such as a spouse and close friends, to make up for our inabilities and incompleteness. If you are not married, you need at least one close friend to be a channel of God's blessing in your life. If you are married, you need other friends in addition to your spouse, because one person cannot fill all your relational needs.

I remember an incident years ago that a counselee shared with me about how his wife blessed him through her caring and friendship one day. Phil, a man in his 30s, had been under intense pressure and stress for several weeks. His new job was a disaster because delays and unreasonable demands from his supervisor were wearing him down. Added to this, Phil and his wife had moved 2000 miles away from home to take this job, and both sets of parents continued to express their displeasure over the move.

On one particular day everything was going wrong at work. On top of work problems, Phil's parents called him at work to dump on him about abandoning them. And as he was walking out at quitting time, his supervisor informed him the he would have to work on Saturday.

When Phil arrived home he was totally dejected. His nonverbal signals screamed discouragement. He told me later, "I felt shattered, discouraged, and unable to please anyone." He immediately headed for his chair and slumped into it in silence.

When Phil's wife came into the room she could read his signals and knew it had not been a good day. Phil explained, "Eileen just came over to me and stood behind me, gently stroking my hair and massaging my stooped shoulders. All she said was, 'Would you like dinner now or later?' and 'Would you like to talk about it or not?' Her sensitivity, her touch, her willingness to give me the freedom to talk or not talk encouraged me so much. I didn't feel all alone anymore. I knew I had someone who would stand by me even in my discouragement. I felt blessed. In fact, I know I am blessed in having such a wife."

In a friendship relationship you will come to a greater understanding of who you are in Christ and as a person. When you engage in intimate sharing and experience transparency, your facades drop away, and you learn to confront who you really are in a new way. One of the blessings of friendship is personal growth and growth as a follower of Christ.

Friendships will help answer your questions and solve your problems. Friends provide a listening ear for each other and assist each other in seeing what they may be blind to by themselves. You no longer feel alone in your struggles, and there is comfort in knowing that someone is standing beside you.[1]

Dr. Archibald Hart describes the value of friendship this way:

> Relationships provide healing, both spiritual and psychological. Spiritual healing and maturity is fostered by those who encourage and affirm us and by those who tutor us in the ways of God. Psychological healing is aided by the laughter and the tears that all good relationships offer. When you feel bruised and beaten, misunderstood and rejected, a true friend is like an oasis in a parched desert. True friendship means that there is someone beside you who cares.[2]

A caring friend conveys the blessing of God's love and care. A helpful friend conveys the blessing of God's commitment to meet our needs. A giving friend conveys the blessing of God's grace and generosity. What a blessing to have friends!

Encouragers—The Balcony People in Life

I overhead a conversation between two men the other day. One man asked his friend, "How do you do it? You've had a lot of adversity this past year, but you seem to keep moving ahead in life instead of getting bogged down in your problems?"

His friend replied, "I guess I could summarize it in one word: encouragement. I have received so much encouragement from other people. Even when I didn't believe in myself, others believed in me and continued to convey their belief in me. When everything seemed to be falling apart, I still knew I was a blessed person, because those around me wouldn't let me think otherwise. It has taught me that I need other people in my life—especially encouragers."

This man isn't alone. Encouragers are the ones who bless us and keep us moving ahead in life. Do you have others who encourage and affirm you? Are you a source of encouragement and affirmation to others? Are you involved with a group of people who are committed to fulfilling 1 Thessalonians 5:11 in each other's lives?: "Therefore encourage one another and build each other up, just as in fact you are doing."

Encouragers have been called "balcony people," because they always seem to be found leaning over the balconies of our lives saying, "You can do it. Go for it. I believe in you. I'm praying for you." Encouragers are conveyors of God's blessing because God Himself is a balcony person. His Word is full of His love and encouragement. And when we become encouragers in the lives of others around us, we are channels of His blessing.

How will you know if you are blessing others with encouragement? You will probably hear people say things like this to you:

• "You listened to me without judging me."
• "You kept telling me that I am a capable person."
• "When I was hurting, you gave me a big hug."
• "When I was honest with you about how I felt, you weren't shocked. I felt so accepted by you."
• "When I was low on faith and hope, you told me you were loaning me your faith and hope until mine returned."

The greatest encouragers in our lives are those who encourage us to grow spiritually. Who is there in your life who prays for you and with you, shares spiritual truth with you, puts you in touch with resources that will equip you spiritually, and helps you develop your spiritual gifts? For whom are you an encourager to spiritual growth? Helping one another grow in the knowledge of God and bear fruit in our lives (Colossians 1:10) is one of the greatest blessings of all.

Beware of the Castle-dwellers and Basement People

Warning: Not everyone in your life will be a source of blessing in your life—even in your church. Some people tend to stand aloof or alienate themselves from others. They never let you get close to them, and they don't want to get close to you. They never let you hug them, and they never put their arms around others—especially in public. They live in isolation and self-imposed solitary confinement much of the time.

These people are like the residents of the medieval castles of several centuries ago. They have erected high walls and water-filled moats around their lives to protect themselves from intimacy. The drawbridge of access remains closed most of the time. They decide who they will allow to enter their lives and just how far they can get in. What they fail to realize is that they have become prisoners of their own defenses. Castle-dwellers are unable to give or receive love from others. Many of them don't even know what blessing they're missing by locking themselves away from others this way.

There are other people who are not just aloof; they are antagonistic. They are described in Proverbs 12:18: "There is one who speaks rashly like the thrusts of a sword" (NASB). These are the people I call "toxic people." They have the unique ability to contaminate relationships instead of bless them. They are also called "basement people." They dwell in dark, damp, dingy basements lying in wait for anyone they can grab and drag down to their dungeon. They are critical. They don't build up; they tear down. They don't build close relationships; they separate friends. They delight in destroying. Sadly, you may have some basement people in your own family. You may feel worn out trying to fend off their negativism.

Fortunately, the Word of God assists us in discovering the kind of people who will be a blessing in our lives and those who will not. We certainly need to minister Christ's love to castle-dwellers and basement people, but we also need healthy, positive, functional people around us who will build us up instead of tear us down.

God's Word expressly instructs us to avoid certain types of basement people because of their negative behavior. Proverbs 22:24-25 states: "Make no friendships with a man given to anger, and with a wrathful man do not associate, lest you learn his ways and get yourself into a snare" (AMP). We are told to avoid those who totally reject the Christian message (Matthew 10:14), those who teach doctrinal error (Matthew 7:6,15), those who are stumbling blocks to young Christians (Matthew 18:6), those who are stubbornly unrepentant (Matthew 18:15-17), and those who are callously unforgiving (Matthew 18:21-35), to name just a few. All through the epistles of the New Testament you will find guidance concerning people in extreme disobedience and rebellion who will not be a blessing to you. We are not to become self-righteous in avoiding them; but we are to be cautious that these basement people do not negatively influence our lives.

Are You Hungry for Blessing?

One of the saddest groups of people I confront in my counseling office are starving people. No, I'm not talking about street people or the homeless. I see people who have nice homes, good incomes, and live with family members. But they are starving because their hunger for the blessing that comes from close, positive relationships is not being fulfilled. Many have sought the blessing of others and been rejected. Others have tried to be people of blessing to others, but their efforts have not been reciprocated. They've been hurt, burned. They still long for the closeness and support of others, but their past experiences keep them locked up in fear.

Do you suffer from this kind of hunger? Are you aware of others around you who are starving for the blessing of relationships? Let your hunger to give and receive blessing override your fear. The hurt you may experience attempting to bless others and receive blessing is not nearly as great as the gnawing inner pain of living in isolation. You *can* develop closeness with others and experience God's blessing through people. It may be a slow journey. It does take time and effort. It does involve a level of discomfort. But it does lead to blessing.

How do relationships develop that have the potential to fill the inner hunger for blessing in our lives? In his book, *We Need Each Other*, Guy Greenfield gives us some helpful direction:

> Reaching the levels of caring, sharing, and intimacy requires commitment, taking the initiative, spending the time, running the risks of rejection, fumbling and embarrassment, and making consistent efforts. Trust is commitment. Sharing your inmost feelings requires a sincere conviction that this is a primary means of developing depth in one's relationships. The deeper levels are not reached accidentally or incidentally but by design and determination. Developing close relationships may even call for sacrifice: giving up the routine of the trivial and going to the trouble of spending time and energy with fellow seekers in the quest for closeness.[3]

Well, who are they? Have you identified the people who are the channels of God's blessing in your life? They're all around you. Even if you haven't fully tapped into the reservoir of blessing in your relationships, the potential is there. Reach out, and let God bless you through others.

❧ P R A Y E R ❧

Dear Lord,

I've been thinking a lot about friends lately. Everybody is talking about relationships, and really knowing each other, but no one seems to do much about it. Or everyone wants to have the same friend—that person who's up in front of the crowd or the gal with the toothpaste smile and the winsome personality. Hardly anyone seems willing to build relationships with ordinary people. You know—the harried housewife with three pre-schoolers, the overweight, under-confident teenager, or the quiet guy on the edge of the crowd. Who was Your friend, Lord? I know You had a lot of acquaintances, and the twelve who shared the ministry, but who was Your friend? I mean the person with whom You could let your hair down. Where You didn't have to watch every word or meet someone's unending expectations. You know, where did You go when You had to get away, but You couldn't bear to be alone again? Was Lazarus that special friend for You, Lord? I think maybe he was. I started to pray, 'Give me a friend like that,' but I thought better of it. Instead I pray, 'Let me be a friend like that.'⁴ In Jesus' Name. Amen.

CHAPTER THIRTEEN

Blessed
to Bless Others

The road was empty, but it wasn't always like this. Most of the time you couldn't travel this road without seeing someone else. But not today. So the traveler kept walking at a brisk pace. This wasn't exactly his neighborhood. In the past he had run into some difficulty with the residents. They didn't care for him or, for that matter, anyone of his race. Prejudice ran deep in the hearts of some of these people. And unfortunately it was often expressed in vicious ways.

Earlier the traveler had paused to rest for a while under a shade tree. That's when he saw two men. One was a minister who didn't say anything to him, didn't even bother to say hello. The traveler thought it strange that a religious man would ignore him. It might have been a good opportunity for him to seek a "convert."

A little later a second man came by, a man who assisted at the church, but he also walked past without saying a word. Perhaps he had a deadline to meet, or there were other reasons why he didn't stop.

When the traveler was well into the countryside, he noticed something lying alongside the road ahead. It was hard to tell what it was at a distance. But as he came closer he could see the whiteness of the flesh. It was a person—a man—and he was naked. He looked like he was dead.

The traveler hurried up to where the man was lying. It was then that he saw the blood. There was blood all over the man's head and chest. His arm was bent at an awkward angle. He was obviously a native to this area, but he was in a bad way. The traveler realized the man had been robbed, beaten, stripped, and left for dead. He looked around, but no one else was in sight. The two men who had passed him earlier were long gone. This was the only way they could have come. Didn't they see this man lying here? They must have. Why didn't they stop and help him?

The traveler didn't even question whether or not he should help the poor victim. He didn't wonder what would happen if someone passing by would think he had beaten the man or if the man died while he was trying to help him. He didn't wonder if the man's relatives would take him to court if he did the wrong thing in trying to help him. The wounded man needed his assistance. The traveler's compassion and concern led him to reach out and help.

The traveler brought some water from a nearby stream and washed the man's wounds. He fashioned a sling for the victim's arm from strips of his tattered clothes. Then the traveler took off his own shirt and covered the man's nakedness. The victim revived and groaned at the intensity of his pain.

Together they hobbled to the next town. People stared at them as they approached. They were a suspicious-looking pair, both half-clothed, both smeared with blood. But the traveler found some people to take him in and provide medical care. Before going on his way, he left some money to cover the medical and housing expenses. He said he would be back in a few days to check on the victim and provide more funds if they were necessary. Then he left.

"The man who brought you here must be a close friend of yours," one of the kind caretakers said. "A stranger wouldn't do what he did."

The injured man replied, "No, I never saw him before. I was mugged and left for dead. He came along and helped me. I too am amazed. Very few people would reach out and help someone like me. Yet he did, even though I'm a Jew and he's a Samaritan. I feel so fortunate. I feel blessed" (see Luke 10:25-37).

Yes, the injured man in Jesus' parable *was* blessed. If it hadn't been for the good Samaritan, he could have died. But there was another person in the story who was blessed. It wasn't the priest or the Levite. They ignored the injured man. They were so closed, self-absorbed, and steeped in religious tradition that they couldn't reach out. They couldn't bless the victim because they were unsure of God's blessing in their lives.

The good Samaritan was blessed. How do I know? Because he blessed others. He was so confident of his relationship to God that he could overlook prejudice, fear, and doubt to become practically and lovingly involved in blessing those around him. That's where our blessing from God meets the road. Knowing that we belong to God is a blessed assurance. But it's not something just for us. We are blessed to bless others.

Where Do I Go from Here?

Perhaps I could introduce this practical side of blessing by anticipating what you're thinking at this stage and then offering my response.

Dear Norm,

I've read the previous chapters, and a number of things are beginning to clear up for me. I'm realizing that I can make some changes in my life, even though

169

it may take some work. I've tried to change before, but I didn't go about it in a way that made any difference. This idea that I need to make a choice to change as a first step is starting to make sense to me.

When you mentioned the yesterday person, I about jumped out of my chair. That described me to a tee, even though I wasn't always aware of it. When I get up in the morning, I am consciously allowing the future to draw me into being different instead of letting the past control me. It's not always comfortable moving ahead, but I am learning to take the risk of being a risk-taker. I know, I know: It's a day by day process, isn't it?

I'm starting to dream more about my life and my future. That's new for me. I was afraid of being a dreamer, but when you put dreams in the context of creating a vision for my life, I realized that positive dreams are possible. And it feels better not to always be a reactor to other people or situations. I can have some say in what happens. I've discovered something that might help others, too. I've learned to take my vision (which I used to call goals) and ask God to reveal His will for me in this direction of my life. It's amazing what I am learning through this process.

Well, that gives you a progress report on my life to this point. But that's not the real reason why I wrote to you. I have a question which I think is practical. I understand that I am a chosen person. I understand that I am a blessed person. But can you give me any other specifics on how being chosen for blessing is going to make a difference in my everyday life? Particularly, what does it mean to the way I relate to the people in my life? For example, how should I relate to the people at work, my neighbors (especially the ones

I wish would move!), my spouse, a controlling parent? I anxiously await your reply.

Yours truly,

A Reader

Many people who have finally grasped the reality that they are chosen for blessing share with me the same testimony and the same questions. Basically they're asking, "Where do I go from here? How does all this fit together?" These are important questions. In these final two chapters I want to share my answers.

More Blessed to Give

Being chosen for blessing means that now is the time for you to learn to live your life in all kinds of circumstances as a person blessed by God. No matter what happens during your day, you must remind yourself that you have been chosen for blessing, even if you just had an accident, lost our job, discovered you have cancer, or suffered a death in the family. These may be strong examples, but they represent the real world. No matter what happens, *you are always a blessed person.* You must learn to think and respond as a blessed person to all people and circumstances in your life. As the apostle Paul put it, "I beg you...to live and act in a way worthy of those who have been chosen for such wonderful blessings as these" (Ephesians 4:1, TLB).

When I hike in the back country of the Grand Teton National Park, I sometimes observe hikers wandering all over the meadow rather than following a specific path. As blessed persons, we are not to be aimless wanderers. We are to stick to the path that has been designed for us by Jesus Christ. His desire is that we live like children of blessing no matter how we feel or what is happening in our life. The beatitudes in Matthew 5:3-12 make this clear. The word "blessed" in these verses can be translated "happy." It is a happiness that goes to the very core of our being. It is the happiness that comes from our desire to please the Father in everything we do.

When we live this way, other people will be blessed. That's the whole idea. You see, blessings are not something for us to keep. They are to be shared with others. They are never to remain with the person who received them. That's where everything we've discussed to this point comes together. You can know all about blessing, but unless it shows in your interactions with others, no one will ever believe that you are blessed.

"How can I be sure God's blessing will be seen in my life?" you ask. Here are some general principles which will apply to everyone.

First, be sure that Jesus Christ is at the center of your life every day. Allow Him to reign supreme in your life (Colossians 1:18). When your roots stretch deeply into His love, you will find that your words and actions around others will reflect His love. It's easy to play favorites with people, even within our families. Being blessed persons, however, means that we will discover a depth of love and acceptance in Christ for all people that we never dreamed possible. I know it's easy to spend more time with the attractive, sharp, and "with it" people, whether at work, in the neighborhood, or even at church. But God loves everyone the same, and so must we.

Next, watch what you say to others (Ephesians 4:29). There is tremendous power in words. They can create emotional wounds or emotional blessings. Most of us get into difficulty more by what we say than anything else. Be sure your words build up rather than tear down. If your words reflect God's grace, people will be drawn to you. Watch what you think about people too, because your thoughts will be reflected in what you say.

When you interact with others, be gentle (Ephesians 4:32). People have fragile egos because of past hurts. Don't let people get under your skin or provoke you. Realize that everyone thinks differently and acts differently, but you can accept them if Christ's love is in you.

Other people are going to disappoint and hurt you. But don't keep score of their wrongs or try to get even with them, even if the hurt is deep. Instead, work out the feelings you have with the Lord, and treat those who hurt you with kindness. People respond positively to someone who can overlook hurt and rejection.

Sometimes we have to put up with those who are unpleasant to be around. In fact, some people are downright obnoxious. But see them as people who are starving for love, kindness, and concern. They need affirmation and acceptance. Allow Jesus Christ to meet their needs through you.

Now, is all this information new? No. Does it work? You bet it does! Did it come from a self-help book? No. Did I make it up? No. Where did it come from? The Bible. It's all scriptural teaching. And these are not mere suggestions. This is the way a blessed person is called to live. Blessing others is not a choice for us as Christians; it's an imperative. We are to respond to others as the Samaritan did to the injured man. Will it change your relationships? Yes!

Becoming a Blessed Blesser

"But how do these principles become a part of my life?" you ask. That's the importance of creating a vision. Begin by personalizing several Bible passages that describe how a blessed person can bless others, passages such as Galatians 5:22-23 (the fruit of the Spirit) or Matthew 5:3-12 (the beatitudes). Write each verse on an index card, and then write four or five different ways you can put that verse into practice with the people in your life. Make some of the ways easy and some more challenging. Each morning spend two or three minutes reading some of the cards aloud. Continue to do this for a month. You will discover a difference.

Becoming a person who blesses others won't happen simply by acting in your own power and resources. It must be through the presence and power of Jesus Christ who lives in you. Everything we do is to be done in the fullness of Jesus Christ. Colossians 3:15-17 instructs us as to how we can equip ourselves with the fullness of Christ.

> Let the peace of Christ rule in your hearts, since as members of one body you were called to peace. And be thankful. Let the word of Christ dwell in you richly as you teach and admonish one another with all wisdom, and as you sing psalms, hymns and spiritual songs with gratitude in your hearts to God. And whatever you do, whether in word or deed, do it all in the name of the Lord Jesus, giving thanks to God the Father through Him.

Let the peace of Christ rule. The peace described here is not just the peace you experience when you have no conflict. It is a sense of wholeness and well-being. When Christ rules, you feel complete. This phrase could be paraphrased, "Let the peace of Christ be umpire in your heart amidst the conflicts of life. Let Christ's peace within decide what is right. Let it be your counselor."

Who or what rules in your life? Perhaps if we allow the peace of Christ to rule in our hearts, the hurtful words we feel like saying in the midst of a conflict would never be said. The indwelling peace of Christ is indispensable to blessing others.

Let the Word of Christ dwell in you. How does God's Word take up residence in us? By reading it, studying it, and memorizing it.

I have seen angry people change because of God's Word.

I have seen frustrated people change because of God's Word.

I have seen anxious people change because of God's Word.

I have seen obnoxious people change because of God's Word.

God's Word changes us. When you read it, ask the Holy Spirit to make it a part of your life.

The truths of Scripture can counter the false beliefs we have about ourselves, God, and others we were taught or have learned in some way. Dr. Kenneth Boa writes:

> The affirmations of Scripture encourage us to walk by faith, not by feelings, and tell us the way things really are regardless of our emotional, cultural, and theological filters. Our circumstances may threaten our commitment to the truths that God is in control of our affairs and has our best interests at heart, but Scripture affirms these foundational principles and tells us to cling to them even in the midst of life's pain.
>
> These affirmations are not a matter of wishful thinking; they are true of every person who places his or her hope in Jesus Christ. They stress our identity in Christ, tell us that process is more important than product, and challenge us to value relationships more than objectives. They teach us that what we do does not determine who we are; rather, our being should shape our doing. They reinforce the realistic perspective that we are aliens and pilgrims, not citizens of this world, and tell us to walk in grace and live in the power of the Spirit of God instead of walking in obedience to a set of external rules and living in the power of the flesh. They counsel us to take the risks of applying biblical precepts and principles and to place our hope in the character and promises of God, and not in the people, possessions, or prestige of this world.[1]

Do all in the name of the Lord Jesus. Everything we do is to be a reflection of Jesus Christ in our lives. And remember that it is! Our obedient, loving behavior reflects Christ's presence. But when we react and respond contrary to the Scriptures and our relationship with Jesus Christ, it reflects that Christ does not fully occupy our life.

Paul's command to do all in the name of the Lord Jesus follows a series of commands in Colossians 3:5-14. He warns us about behaviors we are to put off, behaviors which do not reflect a chosen person. He tells us to get rid of sexual immorality, impurity, lust, evil desires, greed, anger, rage, malice, slander, filthy language, and lying (vv. 5-9). None of these behaviors reflect the presence of Christ in our lives. They are part of our old life without Christ, not our new life with Him. Ridding ourselves of them will prepare us to do all in the name of Christ.

We are to replace these negative behaviors with responses that clearly exemplify that we know Christ: compassion, kindness, humility, gentleness, patience, forgiveness (vv. 10-14). How do you see these qualities reflected in your relationships? To help you create a vision of these responses becoming active and alive in your life, complete the following statements in writing on index cards. Write a separate card for each appropriate person: spouse, parent, child, employer/employees, etc. Read the cards aloud to yourself every day for two weeks:

> The way in which I see myself expressing compassion to ＿＿＿＿＿＿ is…
>
> The way in which I see myself expressing kindness to ＿＿＿＿＿＿ is…
>
> The way in which I see myself expressing humility to ＿＿＿＿＿＿ is…
>
> The way in which I see myself expressing gentleness to ＿＿＿＿＿＿ is…

The way in which I see myself expressing patience to _____ is...

Years ago I was preaching in an evening service on the subject of kindness. I asked everyone in the congregation to write out how they saw themselves being kind to their family members during the coming week. Then I asked several people to stand and share their written response with the entire congregation.

I will never forget the response of one mother who stood and said, "This week I will show kindness to my children by speaking to them as nicely as I speak to the neighbor's children." Have you ever heard 300 people swallow hard with conviction? She hit the nail on the head in a very practical way. But that's the way Scripture is to be lived out in our lives!

There are many other passages you can dwell on that will have a refining quality in your life. Remember: To dwell on Scripture means to reside in it, to think about, to make it truly your own, and to consider how you will express it in your life.

I'm sure by now you are thinking that it's a great deal of work to prepare yourself to bless others. True, but the Christian life is a process of growth that requires conscious, diligent effort. How much time and effort do we spend preparing for a career, building or refurbishing a home, or maintaining our recreational pursuits? If we invested a tenth of the time we spend watching television equipping ourselves to bless others, we would see some dramatic changes in our relationships. There would be many more good Samaritans on the road. Think about it.

❧ *P R A Y E R* ❧

Dear Lord,

Thank You for choosing me, for giving me an inheritance, and for providing power, grace, and access to You.

May my life reflect the truth of Your Word in the ways I interact with others. Help me be diligent in applying Your Word and discovering how life-changing it is. May I draw others to You in whatever I do.

I need Your strength to be compassionate, kind, humble, gentle, patient, and forgiving. I struggle with being consistent in these areas, but I know growth is possible through You.

In Jesus' name. Amen.

CHAPTER FOURTEEN

Keeping Blessing in Perspective

There are many ways we can be good Samaritans to other people as chosen, blessed persons. All of them require that we take the "perspective of positive selection" in our relationships. You may not have heard of this term, but you have probably heard of the concept. Every one of us selects what we choose to focus on in any circumstance. For example, one person looks at a rose bush and sees only sharp thorns. Another person looks at the same bush and sees the beautiful flowers. One person drives into a farm-yard and concentrates on the pigpen with its annoying smell. Another individual focuses on the size and condition of the pigs and their economic value. Each of these observations involves a choice of what the person will focus upon.

Similarly, in our relationships every one of us selects what we will focus on. For example, when a couple first begins courting, they refuse to see anything wrong in each other. They just overlook each other's faults and choose to focus on their positive qualities. Unfortunately, this process often reverses after they marry. They stop choosing to look at each other's strengths and focus on each other's weaknesses. This leads to disappointment, despair, and in some cases total disillusionment in the marriage.

Choosing to Encourage and Affirm

We make the same kinds of choices in our relation-ships with friends, co-workers, spouse, parents, children. The Perspective of Positive Selection, which reflects the principles in God's Word, dictates that we choose to focus on the positive traits in people. This doesn't mean that we are oblivious to or deny the problems or faults in others. Rather we simply decide to focus on their strengths and likable traits. What you choose to concentrate on will determine your attitudes, feelings, and behavior toward others. Your positive focus will also help you reclassify or reinterpret perceived defects in others which may in real-ity simply be differences.

One of the areas where we need to make positive choices and responses is in how we label people. Some-times we make the wrong choice, and people go away deflated instead of blessed. For example, if you sat in on some of my counseling sessions with married couples, you might hear one spouse say to the other, "You are so dense on this issue!" Then you might hear me say to that person, "If I were to say to you 'You are so dense!' how would it make you feel?" The person would probably respond, "I guess I wouldn't like it. And you're probably trying to make me understand that my spouse doesn't like it either." They quickly get the point.

A positive choice requires that we talk to people in such a way that they can hear us, be affirmed by what we say, consider our request, and respond openly and honestly. You *can* request others to change, but your presentation needs to carry with it encouragement and affirmation. For example, the positive side of "You are so dense!" might be "You are deep and thoughtful about many issues."

Many of our labels are critical. I've heard individuals call their spouse or child messy, perfectionistic, clumsy, dependent, dominating, slow, etc. Whenever you label someone and his ability, be careful to be truthful, accurate, and positive. You can be truthful without being damaging or inflammatory in your choice of words. For example you might say the following:

To a messy person
"You like a casual environment."

To the perfectionist
"You really like cleanliness and order."

To the clumsy person
"Among your many skills are a few that are still being developed."

To the dependent person
"You like to encourage others to make decisions and take charge."

To the dominating person
"You enjoy making things happen and taking charge."

To a slow person
"You are very methodical."

To a liberal person
"You are broad-minded, fair to all."

To a quiet person
"You measure your words carefully and put ample thought behind your statements."

To a talkative person
"You are friendly and communicative."

To an argumentative person
"You really love a good, lively discussion."

Your husband leaves quite early for work and doesn't wake you to tell you good-bye. If this is not his normal pattern, you could feel slighted and ignored. How can you relabel this situation to affirm your husband and give him the benefit of the doubt? You might say, "You were considerate this morning by letting me sleep longer and not disturbing me." Then talk to him about how much you like hearing him tell you good-bye before he leaves.

Your wife gets up early each morning to exercise before leaving for work. The noise of the exercise bike in the other room disturbs you. Your wife seems inconsiderate of your desire to sleep in. Relabel the situation by saying, "I'm glad you're concerned enough about your health to stay in shape." Then make some positive suggestions about other times she can ride the bike.

What about you? Are any of these examples uncomfortably familiar? Do the people in your life hear what you say, feel affirmed, consider your requests, and feel free to respond openly and honestly?

There are times when people do need to be admonished and corrected. But the messages you give at such a time need to be positive and affirmative. For example:

• "Have you considered trying it this way? You might like it better."

• "It sounds like it's hard for you to accept a compliment. Perhaps you need more practice accepting them, and I need more practice giving them."

• "I'm not sure I communicated in a way that made it easy for you to hear. Let me say it again, then you tell me what you heard."

• "I would appreciate it if you wouldn't do that again. But here is something you *can* do."

• "I wonder about the choice you made. Here are some other possibilities for you to consider."

Accentuate the Positive

What others really need to hear from us are affirming statements that reflect the fact that we feel affirmed and blessed by God. Here are a few examples:

- "You respond to others at work so well. You have such patience."
- "You have a wonderful ability for..."
- "Thank you for taking time to pick up the cleaning for me."
- "Your cooking has become even better over the last year."
- "I liked the way you straightened my closet for me."

But our affirmation of others should not only be centered on what they do but on who they are. Our affirmations need to reflect the way God affirms us. His love is not based on our merit or anything we have done or will do. He simply loves and accepts us. Others need that same response from us as well. For example:

- "You're a very special person to me."
- "I'm so glad you are in our family. You make it special."
- "I love you because you deserve to be loved. You don't have to earn it."
- "You make my life more complete just by being you."
- "I'm glad I found you as a friend."
- "Have I ever told you that..."

Affirmations show that you not only care about and recognize people for who they are and what they have done, but your positive comments encourage others to continue on that pathway and grow!

There are many other ways to encourage and affirm your spouse, parent, child, friend, and co-workers both verbally and nonverbally. Here are some additional ways you can pass on blessings to another.

- Bring these people before God in prayer and thank Him for each specific quality or trait you have discovered in them. Ask Him to bless them and make their day better than yesterday.

- Endeavor to make their day and workload easier and not create more work for them to do.
- Stop a behavior on your part that distracts from their well-being.
- Draw out their positive qualities in public, and purposely avoid embarrassing them.
- Give them both the closeness and the space they need to grow and recuperate from the pressures of life.
- Encourage them to grow even when it threatens and challenges you to grow, since you have to change also.
- Encourage and support these people in participating in their favorite wholesome activities, even when you can't understand how anyone would ever enjoy it!
- Listen to their perception of issues without immediately giving your opinion or becoming defensive.
- Learn methods of resolving differences and working toward harmony rather than just avoiding or postponing conflict.
- Try to understand their personality differences, and adjust your responses to respect and honor each person's uniqueness.
- Be willing to grow as a person to avoid stagnation in your relationship with others.

Are you a valued person? Yes, you are. When we value others through our words, we bless them. Words of encouragement, praise, acceptance, affirmation, and belief in others are a blessing and a way we show value to them.

Change Is Possible—Believe It!

There is another way to respond to others that will evidence the fact that we are people for blessing. The risk factor for this response is a bit higher than for choosing to affirm others, but the results are well worth the risk. It's choosing to believe that another person will respond differently even when his track record is not so positive.

Believe that your spouse, parent, child, friend, or co-worker will be different in the future. Believe in them as God believes in you!

I remember a couple I counseled one day, Sue and Jim. As they sat in my office we talked about their pattern of communication. Their conversation was a classic example of mutually disabling distrust.

Sue said, "I can tell from Jim's short, terse comments and his scowls that he's upset with me. But when I ask him, 'What's wrong?' all I get is, 'Nothing is wrong.'"

I asked Jim, "What should Sue do when she senses something is wrong between you?"

"She should just ask me," Jim said.

"But she just said she does ask you, and you say nothing," I responded. "Something is usually wrong when she confronts you, isn't it?"

Jim answered, "Yes, I'm usually upset about how she's getting after the kids."

"Jim, why not tell her how you feel since you are showing it anyway?" Then I turned to Sue and said, "Sue, just ask him each time, 'What's wrong?'"

Sue started to counter with, "But all he's said in the past is..."

I interrupted her. "Could you tell Jim what he will be hearing from you in the future?"

She caught on. "Jim," she said, "when I sense that something is wrong, I will ask you, and I believe that, from now on, you will be more open about telling me what's wrong. And each time you do open up to me, I will thank you for it."

"That would be great," Jim said. "I can handle that. And I sure like hearing from you that you believe I'll be different. I will tell you what I'm feeling. And even when I don't know what I'm feeling, I'll tell you that too. But don't criticize my feelings like you've done..."

I interrupted Jim. "Jim, instead of talking about the past, tell Sue what you believe she will do in the future."

"You're right," he said. "I was going to condemn Sue before anything ever happened because of what's happened before. Sue, I believe that when I share my feelings with you, you'll listen to me and thank me for sharing. Then we can work toward a solution."

When you believe in the potential of another person changing, you are blessing them.

Communicating a Blessed Future

In the book *The Blessing,* the authors suggest another way by which people chosen for blessing can bless others: picturing a special future them. You have probably done this with others even though you may not be aware of it. For example, parents often do this with their children in a negative way by making comments like, "No one will want to go out with a fat boy like you" or "Don't waste your time; I doubt that you'll make it to college." These are words of prediction. Negative words like these convey a future to the child. And unfortunately, if they're repeated often enough, sometimes they become reality in the child's life.

But when someone hears words that imply a special future for them, their attitude about life and the future can be affected positively. Affirming the positive traits you see in a child or adult and predicting something good that will grow from them in their future is a blessing.

In the Old Testament we have an example of this as Isaac spoke to his son, Jacob: "May God give you of heaven's dew and of earth's richness—an abundance of grain and new wine. May nations serve you and peoples bow down to you. Be lord over your brothers, and may the sons of your mother bow down to you. May those who curse you be cursed and those who bless you be blessed" (Genesis 27:28-29). In these words Isaac painted a verbal picture of a fulfilling future that gave Jacob security in knowing that he had something to look forward to.

What would your life be like today if you heard consistently positive statements about your qualities as you grew into adulthood? It helps when other people believe in us. God does this. One of my favorite verses comes from the prophet Jeremiah, who assures us of the special future we have with God: "For I know the thoughts that I think toward you, says the Lord, thoughts of peace and not of evil, to give you a future and a hope" (29:11, NKJV).

Jesus described a hopeful future for His disciples:

"In My Father's house are many mansions; if it were not so, I would have told you. I go to prepare a place for you. And if I go and prepare a place for you, I will come again and receive you to Myself; that where I am, there you may be also" (John 14:2-3, NKJV).

The emphasis in speaking about a positive future is on becoming. True statements of becoming are in line with Scripture: "We confidently and joyfully look forward to actually becoming all that God has in mind for us to be" (Romans 5:2, TLB). I like way Dr. Archibald Hart describes this process:

> That word *becoming* is a beautiful word, pregnant with associations and images. It implies *direction* in our growth, showing that there is purpose and great potential in the future. I begin my "becoming" by claiming the freedom to be the individual I am and accepting and affirming my uniqueness. But I also place myself at the disposal of my Creator and Savior so that I can fulfill His divine plan for my life.
>
> As a little child, I kept silkworms for a hobby; most kids in my town did. We traded squares of blotting paper with worm eggs laid on them every springtime and prepared ventilated shoe boxes with mulberry leaves to receive the little worms as they hatched.

Every day we fed them fresh leaves until they were large and ready to spin their cocoons. These other worms seemed to be ugly and useless. They ate the leaves so that the plants became ugly and even died. As a child I wondered why God even put them there!

But then the miracle happened. The worms, hidden in their cocoons for many long weeks, suddenly emerged, revealing the wonder of metamorphosis. And then came the surprise. Our silkworms became moths, and the ugly garden caterpillars became beautiful butterflies!

Granted the silk moths were not as colorful as the butterflies, but on the way they had produced the most beautiful patterns you can imagine as they wove their tiny thread of silk around any shape cardboard form you left in the box. Hearts, squares, and circles became covered in pretty silk. The butterflies, on the other hand, wove their silky beauty right into their colorful wings. It almost seemed that the uglier the caterpillar, the prettier the butterfly![1]

There are those who may appear as ugly to you as a caterpillar. But all it takes is someone like you with words of belief in that person to help the butterfly unfold.

For a number of years I showed a film to my seminary classes called *Johnny Lingo*. It's the simple story of a south seas islander who wanted to marry the chief's daughter. The custom was to pay the father a number of cows based upon the girl's beauty.

Unfortunately, this father wasn't expecting much, because his daughter was quite plain. But when Johnny Lingo came to call on him and ask for her hand, he brought 10 cows with him. Everyone, including the father, thought Johnny was out of his mind to pay such a high price for this girl. But Johnny was insistent, so the bargain was made. The couple rode off in their boat for an extended honeymoon on another island.

When they returned everyone was stunned. The chief's daughter had turned into a beautiful woman. The father asked Johnny Lingo, "What happened to my daughter that she turned into such a beautiful woman?"

He said, "I simply treated her as a 10-cow woman, and when she heard what had been paid for her, she saw herself in a new light."

It's a simple and humorous story, but I have never forgotten it. How you treat others can affect how they see themselves years later.

Blessing the Hard-to-Bless

Now let's consider blessing people you might want to avoid. We all know them. Who are they? Problem people, people who are difficult to get along with. Some of them you would rather not even know! Some you wish would go away, but they don't. Some of them don't even change much. That's all right. See them as defective if you want to. But realize that we're all defective in some way. You must learn to see problem people as opportunities for blessing others. You must take charge of how you think about them and respond to them. This is your opportunity to respond as a person chosen for blessing!

Denying these people and what they do will not work.

Denying how you feel about them will not work.

Thinking negative thoughts about them or ruminating about unpleasant experiences with them will not work.

Running from them will not work and is often impossible.

Responding to them with words and deeds of blessing *will* work.

189

Start with a Vision

"How can I bless the people in my life, including the problem people?" you ask. "Where do I start?" By creating a new vision for how you will respond to people.

First, identify the person you would like to respond to in a new way. Who is this person? How would you like to respond differently? Do you pray specifically for this person each day? If so, in what way?

Next, on a sheet of paper describe in detail how you see yourself thinking, speaking, and behaving toward this individual in the future. See yourself as a positive, balanced person who is not fearful, intimidated, or overbearing toward this individual. See yourself becoming satisfied and content with the way in which you are responding. Do not place the emphasis on how the other person responds. Your concern is not to change him but to let your life reflect before him who you are in Jesus Christ.

The next step is very important. It will help you as you pray and meditate on the Scriptures and grow in your understanding of being chosen for blessing and chosen to bless others. Your daily, intimate fellowship with Him is indispensable. This exercise will help you focus in on how Jesus Christ is responding to your desire.

Find a quiet place alone, away from anything that might distract you. You may need to put a "Do not disturb" sign on the door and be sure the phone is off the hook.

Relax for a moment. Reflect on what you have learned about yourself and your relationship with God in the earlier chapters of this book. Accept the fact that you do not have to remain a yesterday person in your relationship with the person you want to bless. Acknowledge that you can be different. You will need to believe that you are a changed person before you can change your actions. Contrary to New Age exercises that encourage people to "visualize" something until it becomes a reality, you are simply acknowledging something God has already accomplished, something you believe about yourself by faith because God said it is true.

You use your imagination every day to grow and solve problems. You mentally rehearse an important conversation you're going to have with your spouse, your boss, or a client. You mentally review events that happened to you so you can determine how to act the next time. Our minds were given to us by God to help us create mental pictures based on God's Word for how we should behave. God doesn't intend for you to think yourself into being a blessed person. You already are blessed; use your God-given imagination to help you see how your blessedness can be lived out in your life and your relationships.

As you think about how you can respond to those you love as a blessed person, quiet your heart so that you can hear the Lord's instruction. As you seek Him, the Holy Spirit will confirm all that you have learned about blessing. His assurances will comfort and strengthen you. It's as though He would say to you, "I came to share something with you, My friend. You are a chosen person. I want you to know and believe that you have been chosen to *receive* blessing and *give* blessing. Because My life is in you, you now have My resources and strength. You *can* give to others. I want you to give of yourself out of My abundance in you. I want you to discover all of the abilities I have deposited in you. I want you to help others discover their gifts too. Do this and you will have a new life. I care for you, and I love you. Bless others and treat them the way I would."

It might be helpful to you, as you spend time with the Lord, to write out your feelings. Often it takes time for deep feelings and thoughts to surface. You might also want to describe in writing the type of person you want to be and the life you now want to live. Pray that God will give you a vision for service to others.

Here are several practical suggestions to give you structure and a definite plan to follow in preparing to bless the people in your life.

1. If you find yourself retreating into the same old pattern of thinking and living toward people, review your time of commitment and the subsequent writing exercise.

2. Read and meditate on the following verses:

I can do everything through him who gives me strength (Philippians 4:13).

Perseverance must finish its work so that you may be mature and complete, not lacking anything (James 1:4).

A new command I give you: Love one another. As I have loved you, so you must love one another (John 13:34).

Carry each other's burdens, and in this way you will fulfill the law of Christ (Galatians 6:2).

You, my brothers, were called to be free. But do not use your freedom to indulge the sinful nature; rather, serve one another in love (Galatians 5:13).

Do nothing out of selfish ambition or vain conceit, but in humility consider others better than yourselves (Philippians 2:3).

Finally, brothers, whatever is true, whatever is noble, whatever is right, whatever is pure, whatever is lovely, whatever is admirable—if anything is excellent or praiseworthy—think about such things. Whatever you have learned or received or heard from me, or seen in me—put it into practice. And the God of peace will be with you (Philippians 4:8-9).

3. Make a complete list of the areas of your life that you would like to see improved in your relationship to others. Continue writing until the list is complete. What is the new vision that you have for being different in these areas?

4. Make another list of the three individuals you are closest to. What are their concerns and needs? If you are not aware of their needs, ask them what their needs are and how you can minister to them in a better way. How can you be a blessing to them?

As you experience these disciplines, you may feel uncomfortable at first. That's quite normal and all right. In time these feelings will diminish, and you will discover a quiet and solid satisfaction as you enter your new lifestyle.[2]

Are you a chosen person? Yes.

Are you a blessed person? Yes.

Are you a person chosen for blessing? Yes! Yes! Yes!

Live life to reflect your blessings.

❦ *P R A Y E R* ❦

Dear Lord,

Here I am at the end of a journey. I'm discovering so much about myself and You. I want to remember all that I need to about You and the life of blessing You have called me to live. I want to praise You for so much I have previously overlooked.

Thank You for the possibilities You see in me.

Thank You for helping me see others in a new way.

Thank You for new ways I have discovered for blessing others.

Thank You for picturing a special future for me.

Thank You for seeing me as a "becoming" person.

Thank You that I am a chosen person.

Thank You that I am a blessed person.

In Jesus' name. Amen.

NOTES

CHAPTER 1

1. J.I. Packer, *Knowing God* (Downers Grove, IL: InterVarsity Press, 1973), p. 37.
2. Myron C. Madden, *Blessing: Giving the Gift of Power* (Nashville, TN: Broadman Press, 1988), p. 33.
3. Ibid, p. 16.
4. "And the Father Will Dance." Lyrics adapted from Zephaniah 3:14,17 and Psalms 54:2,4. Arranged by Mark Hayes.
5. John Piper, *The Pleasures of God* (Portland, OR: Multnomah Press, 1991), p. 188.
6. Ibid, p. 195.

CHAPTER 2

1. *English Ritual* (Collegeville, MN: The Liturgical Press, 1964), pp. 369-370.
2. Ibid, p. 457.
3. *The Methodist Hymnal* (Nashville, TN: The Methodist Publishing Co., 1939), adapted from p. 519.
4. Ralf Garborg, *The Family Blessing* (Dallas, TX: Word Publishing, 1987), adapted from pp. 11-12.
5. Colin Brown, ed., *New International Dictionary of New Testament Theology* (Grand Rapids, MI: Zondervan Publishers, 1975), p. 211.
6. Lloyd John Ogilvie, *Lord of the Impossible* (Nashville, TN: Abingdon Press, 1984), p. 28.
7. Ibid, pp. 28-29.
8. Roger C. Palms, *Enjoying the Closeness of God* (Minneapolis, MN: World Wide Publications, 1989), p. 246.
9. Thomas Kelly, *A Testament of Devotion* (New York: Harper and Row, 1941), p. 25.

CHAPTER 3

1. H. Norman Wright, *Recovering from the Losses of Life* (Terrytown, NY: Fleming H. Revell, 1991), adapted from pp. 142-143.
2. Linda Rich, "No One" (Assigned to Inter-Varsity Christian Fellowship of the USA, 1970), used by permission.
3. David C. Needham, *Birthright* (Portland, OR: Multnomah Press, 1979), adapted from pp. 127-129.

CHAPTER 4

1. Pat Springle, *Rapha's 12-Step Program for Overcoming Dependency* (Houston, TX: Rapha Publishing, 1990), adapted from p. 23.
2. Ibid, adapted from pp. 22-23.
3. William and Kristi Gaultiere, *Mistaken Identity* (Old Tappan, NJ: Fleming H. Revell, 1989), p. 56.
4. Ibid, adapted from pp. 183-186.

CHAPTER 5

1. Ken Gire, *Incredible Moments With the Savior* (Grand Rapids, MI: Zondervan Publishers, 1990), p. 84.
2. Dr. Sidney Simon, *Getting Unstuck* (New York: Warner Books, 1988), adapted from p. 14.
3. Lloyd John Ogilvie, *Lord of the Impossible* (Nashville, TN: Abingdon Press, 1984), pp. 129-130.
4. Jack W. Hayford, *Taking Hold of Tomorrow* (Ventura, CA: Regal Books, 1989), p. 33.
5. Ibid, p. 33.
6. Ibid, adapted from pp. 39-46.

CHAPTER 6

1. Leonard Felder, *A Fresh Start* (New York: Signet Books, 1987), adapted from p. 8.
2. Ibid, adapted from pp. 25-26.
3. John W. James and Frank Cherry, *The Grief Recovery Handbook* (San Francisco, CA: Harper and Row, 1988), adapted from p. 7.

4. H. Norman Wright, *Always Daddy's Girl* (Ventura, CA: Regal Books, 1989), adapted from pp. 205-224.

CHAPTER 7

1. Leonard Felder, *A Fresh Start* (New York: Signet Books, 1987), adapted from p. 8.
2. Ibid, adapted from pp. 25-26.
3. John W. James and Frank Cherry, *The Grief Recovery Handbook* (San Francisco, CA: Harper and Row, 1988), adapted from p. 7.
4. H. Norman Wright, *Always Daddy's Girl* (Ventura, CA: Regal Books, 1989), adapted from pp. 205-224.

CHAPTER 8

1. Tim Hansel, *Holy Sweat* (Waco, TX: Word Books, 1987), p. 74.
2. David Viscott, *Risking* (New York, NY: Pocket Books, 1977), adapted from pp. 18-21, 28.
3. Dr. Sidney Simon, *Getting Unstuck* (New York: Warner Books, 1988), adapted from pp. 175-179.
4. Lloyd John Ogilvie, *Lord of the Impossible* (Nashville, TN: Abingdon Publishers, 1984), p. 9.
5. Roger C. Palms, *Enjoying the Closeness of God* (Minneapolis, MN: Publisher?, 1989), p. 115.

CHAPTER 9

1. Tim Hansel, *Holy Sweat* (Waco, TX: Word Books, 1987), p. 55.

CHAPTER 10

1. Ken Gire, *Incredible Moments with the Savior* (Grand Rapids, MI: Zondervan Publishers, 1990), pp. 22-23.
2. Bob George, *Growing in Grace* (Eugene, OR: Harvest House Publishers, 1991), p. 128.
3. Robert Veninga, *A Gift of Hope* (Boston, MA: Little Brown and Co., 1985), p. 11.

4. Barry L. Johnson, *Choosing Hope* (Nashville, TN: Abingdon Press, 1988), p. 15.
5. Ibid, p. 77.

CHAPTER 11

1. Ann Kaiser Stearns, *Coming Back* (New York: Ballantine Books, 1989), adapted from pp. 193-195.
2. Lloyd Ogilvie, *Lord of the Impossible* (Nashville, TN: Abingdon Press, 1984), p. 20.
3. Stearns, *Coming Back*, adapted from pp. 220-255.

CHAPTER 12

1. Archibald Hart, *Fifteen Principles for Achieving Happiness* (Waco, TX: Word Publishers, 1988), adapted from p. 150.
2. Ibid, p. 15.
3. Guy Greenfield, *We Need Each Other* (Grand Rapids, MI: Baker Book House, 1984), p. 35.
4. Richard Exley, *Life's Bottom Line* (Tulsa, OK: Honor Books, 1990), pp. 249,250.

CHAPTER 13

1. Kenneth Boa, *Night Light* (Brentwood, TN: Wolgemuth and Hyatt Publishers, Inc., 1989), p. 2.

Other Good
Harvest House Reading

QUIET TIMES FOR COUPLES
by *H. Norman Wright*

Noted counselor and author Norm Wright provides the help you need to nurture your oneness in Christ. In a few moments together each day you will discover a deeper, richer intimacy with each other and with God, sharing your fondest dreams and deepest thoughts—creating memories of quiet times together.

HOLINESS AND THE SPIRIT OF THE AGE
by *Floyd McClung*

A penetrating look at what it means to be holy in an unholy world. Holiness is not a matter of conforming to a set of outward rules; it is a matter of being passionate in our relationship with the Father—set free to live lives that are *truly* pleasing to Him!

SILENT STRENGTH FOR MY LIFE
by *Lloyd John Ogilvie*

Gladness...refreshment...encouragement...renewal... these are the rich rewards of quiet time spent with God. Daily time spent with God, alone in His presence, satisfied by His Word, makes our hearts stronger and our vision clearer. *Silent Strength* is designed to help you maximize your time with our Lord. As we glimpse His power, we find ourselves ready to meet the challenges of the day with a strength that is beyond our own, a silent strength that comes from God alone.

GOD'S BEST FOR MY LIFE
by *Lloyd John Ogilvie*

Not since Oswald Chambers' *My Utmost for His Highest* has there been such an inspirational yet easy-to-read devotional. Dr. Ogilvie provides guidelines for maximizing your prayer and meditation time.

A PASSION FOR GOD'S PRESENCE
by *Wayne Jacobsen*

Clothed in expensive architecture, elaborate programs, and impressive statistics, the modern church has all too often traded the presence of God for the nakedness of religious form. Jacobsen gives a clear and inspiring view of what true intimacy with God entails and offers a blueprint that every person can use to build that intimacy.